3 IN 1

KIRSTIN RAE EVANS

BODY
LANGUAGE

BONUS INSIDE

Analyze Expressions, Understand Behaviors, and Influence Situations by Using Physical Cues

73 TECHNIQUES & TIPS
for Reading People Through the Art of Nonverbal Communication

TABLE OF CONTENTS

INTRODUCTION

B ody language is universal, silently speaking volumes about our thoughts, feelings, and intentions. Without saying a word, our gestures, facial expressions, and posture convey messages that shape how others perceive us and how we understand them. Yet, in a world teeming with unspoken cues, many grapple with a significant challenge: *the inability to read and interpret physical cues accurately.*

Communication is a complex tapestry woven together with verbal and nonverbal threads. While words carry explicit meaning, it is often the subtle nuances of body language that truly reveal what lies beneath the surface. Understanding and responding to these nonverbal cues is paramount to effective communication and building meaningful connections.

However, the struggle to decode and utilize body language cues is a prevalent issue that hinders our interpersonal interactions. Many individuals are at a loss when faced with a sea of physical signals, unable to interpret the intentions, emotions, or hidden messages conveyed through gestures, facial expressions, or postures.

Subsequently, navigating the intricate landscape of body language becomes even harder in social settings. Picture a bustling party filled with animated conversations, laughter, and people exchanging glances. In this lively atmosphere, being proficient in reading and responding to body language cues becomes essential. Unfortunately, the challenges of understanding body language in social environments can be overwhelming. The inability to discern social cues can result in missed opportunities, strained relationships, or embarrassing misunderstandings. In these moments, the importance of body language becomes apparent, as it shapes our interactions and influences how others perceive us.

Nevertheless, whether a missed business opportunity at a networking event or misinterpreting romantic interest on a first date, the consequences of misreading body language can have a lasting impact on various aspects of our lives. Fortunately, acquiring and improving body language skills is similar to learning an instrument or riding a bike, as they can be developed with practice and dedication. By studying the theory behind body language and applying it in real-life situations, you can enhance your communication abilities and better understand the thoughts and emotions of those around you.

Mastering body language can bring life-changing benefits in various aspects of life, including career advancement, improved social interactions, and even finding a romantic partner. First impressions often rely on nonverbal cues such as facial expressions, posture, and hand gestures, which can influence how others perceive you. This book will discuss these three fundamental elements of body language to provide a comprehensive understanding that can positively impact your personal and professional life.

While the theory of body language may be straightforward, putting it into practice can be challenging, especially in dynamic social environments. Body language is context-dependent, and interpreting it accurately requires considering numerous factors. Consequently, consistently practicing these techniques to refine your skills is essential.

Developing body language skills does not necessitate altering your personality. Both introverts and extroverts can benefit from understanding and using body language effectively. Introverts, for example, can excel in understanding and utilizing body language effectively, as they are often more attentive to nonverbal cues and excel in active listening. Although this book concentrates on body language, other factors, such as conversational skills and active listening, contribute to effective communication are covered. Combining these elements with body language techniques can lead to more successful interactions, creating a whole greater than the sum of its parts.

Book 1:
Reading Between the Lines:

Mastering the Unspoken —
Enhancing Communication and
Influence Through Facial Expressions

Kirsten Rae Evans

TABLE OF CONTENTS

INTRODUCTION

In this book, we will explore facial expressions and their impact on building rapport and influencing others. Enhancing your ability to read facial expressions contributes to a deeper understanding of your conversation partner's emotions, allowing you to adjust your approach or continue a successful conversation.

Simultaneously, comprehending others' facial expressions leads to increased self-awareness regarding your expressions, ensuring inappropriate nonverbal cues do not hinder your conversational skills. Furthermore, we will delve into emotional contagion —the phenomenon where our emotions influence others— and discuss how to use it to foster cooperation and positive feelings, improve your leadership skills, and open new career opportunities.

Before diving into these topics, discover the science behind the human brain's function, focusing on facial recognition and processing, which are prioritized from a young age. This foundation will provide a better understanding of the significance of facial expressions in communication and interpersonal relationships.

CHAPTER 1

FACIAL EXPRESSIONS

Facial expressions are one of the biggest ways we, as humans, communicate. Our capacity for facial recognition and processing underpins our success as a species, firmly establishing humans as social, cooperative beings. In this chapter, we look at the science surrounding facial recognition.

The Brain and Faces

Instantly after birth, a baby's gaze is drawn to faces. A newborn will look more at other people's faces than they will look at other objects. In fact, psychologists from Emory University have found that different parts of an infant's brain are at work when looking at people or places. Meanwhile, babies start to recognize particular faces—such as their mother's or father's face—at as young an age as two months. This corresponds with the findings of psychologists from the Massachusetts Institute of Technology, who find that the area of the brain dedicated to identifying human faces is functional from two months. These findings prove that the human brain prioritizes facial recognition from a very young age and may come with settings "pre-installed" for recognizing and processing faces.

The human brain has a dedicated area of the brain for facial recognition, known as the fusiform face area (FFA). While your brain processes most objects with the lateral occipital complex (LOC), the FFA focuses on fine-grain distinctions between otherwise similar objects. It is critical for recognizing different faces but can also be seen at work in experts who rely on similarly complex differentiations. For example, a dedicated birdwatcher will use the FFA when distinguishing different species of birds, while the average individual will only use the LOC. In this sense, the universal use of the FFA for human faces suggests that we are all "face experts."

Some psychologists believe that facial recognition is not only prioritized in the development of the brain but is an innate ability present from birth. Psychologists from the Istituto Italiano di Tecnologia suggest infants "exhibit an extraordinary sensitivity to face-like stimuli" within minutes of birth. This evidence gives rise to the dominant theory of facial recognition: the view that the neonate brain "contains an innate face detection device, dubbed 'Conspec.'"

Sensitivity to faces is a fundamental part of what it is to be human. As such, it explains the phenomenon of *pareidolia*: our tendency to see patterns where they do not exist. Humans are very prone to seeing faces in objects. You might look at the front grill of a car and see a smiling face or look at a European-style plug and see a face in shock. For example, due to pareidolia, you probably see a face in the image below:

Indeed, the phenomenon of pareidolia probably underpinned early emoticons using text such as ":). " Because our brains are hardwired to see faces everywhere, we quickly recognize a colon and a round bracket as smiling faces.

The FFA takes a holistic approach, finding patterns and relations between visual stimuli. Subsequently, the brain processes the relations between those parts that make up the face. If two objects are on either side of a bigger object, the FFA is predisposed to process them as ears. Meanwhile, if two objects are vaguely parallel with the "ears" in the middle of the bigger object, the FFA processes them as eyes, and so on. This fundamental face template is used to quickly recognize faces, enabling social cohesion that allowed the early human race to work together and thrive.

Furthermore, the connection between body language and developing interpersonal skills lies in the brain's remarkable ability to process and recognize faces. Facial expressions are a powerful tool for establishing rapport, with our brains instinctively paying close attention to them. When used effectively, facial expressions can significantly enhance social interactions; however, inappropriate expressions may harm communication.

The Universal Guide to Facial Expressions

Despite the importance of facial expressions in human interaction today, the University of Toronto neuroscientist Daniel H. Lee argues that facial expressions were not originally tools of communication (Lee et al., 2014). Instead, Lee finds that our facial expressions arise from natural reactions to light and other environmental stimuli.

For example, suppose that you are feeling scared. A normal facial expression of fear involves wide, open eyes. This gives a broader visual field and allows light to hit your eyes, which is adaptive for early humans alert for physical threats. By contrast, suppose you feel disgusted by something. This is typified by your eyes being pinched and your nose wrinkled, reducing the light meeting your eyes but improving your visual focus.

From there, these universally adaptive facial expressions became communicative shorthands for the associated emotions. Because it is adaptive to have wide eyes when frightened, we learned to associate wide eyes with fright, and facial expressions played a communication role.

This theory of the development of facial expressions suggests extraordinary universality in human facial expressions. Paul Ekman, a professor of psychology at the University. Despite the importance of facial expressions in human interaction today, they were not originally communication tools. Instead, our facial expressions arose from natural reactions to light and other environmental stimuli. For example, suppose that you are feeling scared. A normal facial expression of fear involves wide, open eyes. This gives a broader visual field and allows more light to hit your eyes, which is adaptive for early humans alert for physical threats. By contrast, suppose you feel disgusted by something. Subsequently, this emotion is typified by your eyes being pinched and your nose wrinkled, reducing the light meeting your eyes but improving your visual focus. These universally adaptive facial expressions evolved into communicative shorthand for corresponding emotions. For instance, wide eyes became associated with fright due to their adaptive nature in such situations, and consequently, this facial expression assumed a communicative function. This theory of the development of facial expressions suggests extraordinary universality in human facial expressions. There are seven universal facial expressions across the human species, which are outlined in detail below:

- **Happiness:** Wrinkles around the eyes, raised cheeks, raised lip corners
- **Sadness:** Inner eyebrow corners raised, loose eyelids, pulled down lip corners
- **Fear:** Eyebrows up and pulled together, upper eyelids pulled up, mouth stretched
- **Disgust:** Eyebrows down, nose wrinkled, upper lip rolled up, lips loose
- **Anger:** Eyebrows down, upper eyelids pulled up and lower eyelids pulled down, lips rolled in or tightened
- **Contempt:** Eyes natural, lips pulled back on one side of the mouth

- **Surprise:** Pulled up eyebrows, pulled up eyelids, mouth hanging open

These facial expressions enable individuals to discern emotions like happiness or fear in people from entirely different cultures, even in distant countries. However, acknowledge that not every element of human facial expressions is universal, nor are facial expressions an entirely culturally specific phenomenon. For instance, various cultures may exhibit unique ways of expressing and perceiving emotions, leading to differences in facial expressions. Hence, getting the basics of facial expression right while being mindful of potential cultural differences when speaking to people of different backgrounds is necessary.

A common cultural difference is found in "display rules," which are a culture's norms for when it is appropriate to show emotions. For example, Japanese social norms hold that showing strong emotions around strangers is inappropriate and that making eye contact with strangers is impolite. By contrast, American social norms permit eye contact with strangers and the expression of strong emotions.

The Science of the Evolution of Facial Expressions

Facial expressions have played an integral role in human evolution, with biological and evolutionary origins dating back to our ancestors. These expressions have served as adaptive functions, allowing humans to convey and interpret emotions, intentions, and social cues. The cross-cultural universality of facial expressions supports the idea that they are innate and instinctual rather than learned behaviors. Numerous studies have provided evidence favoring the universality hypothesis, demonstrating that facial expressions are universally recognized and understood across different cultures.

The link between facial expressions and emotions is a fascinating area of research. The facial feedback hypothesis suggests that facial expressions can influence our emotional experiences. When we make specific facial expressions, it triggers corresponding emotional states. Additionally, expressive behaviors exhibited through facial expressions provide valuable insights into an individual's emotional state and intentions.

Theoretical foundations by eminent scientists like Charles Darwin and Paul Ekman propose that facial expressions are a primordial form of communication. Darwin emphasized the importance of facial expressions in human evolution, considering them biologically advantageous for survival. Paul Ekman's extensive research on universal facial expressions further supported this theory, revealing that certain facial expressions are universally recognized and displayed across different cultures.

From comparative studies with non-human primates, scientific evidence supports facial expressions as a primordial communication system. Similarities in facial expressions and emotional recognition between humans and non-human primates suggest a shared evolutionary heritage. Cross-cultural studies on emotional recognition have also shown that facial expressions are universally understood, indicating their deep-seated and instinctual nature.

Moreover, facial expressions provide an evolutionary advantage in communication due to their ability to transmit information rapidly. These expressions can swiftly convey emotions and intentions, enabling efficient communication even without language. Furthermore, facial expressions facilitate emotional contagion and social bonding, allowing individuals to empathize and connect emotionally.

Aside from that, facial expressions serve as the foundation of nonverbal communication, complementing and enhancing verbal language. Neuroscientific studies have shed light on the intricate mechanisms of facial expression recognition, showing distinct neural pathways dedicated to processing and interpreting facial cues. Additionally, evolutionary psychology suggests that facial expressions played a significant role in language development, as they provided a means for early humans to convey and understand emotions before the emergence of complex verbal communication.

Language acquisition involves the integration of facial expressions and vocal cues. Infants learn to associate facial expressions with specific emotions and vocalizations, forming a cohesive understanding of communication. This integration highlights the integral role of facial expressions in language development and the seamless coordination between nonverbal and verbal aspects of communication. In the present day, facial expressions have a powerful impact on interpersonal interaction between human beings.

The Utility of Facial Expressions

The significance of facial expressions in the human experience is evident, as they are deeply ingrained in our neural structures. Our perception of facial expressions is typically an instantaneous process that occurs without conscious effort to memorize a face. This innate ability allows us to instinctively identify someone we have previously encountered, recognizing their familiarity even if we cannot recall their name or the context of our last meeting.

During conversations, we unconsciously rely on automatic processes to interpret facial expressions. The human face has a remarkable capacity for expressing emotions, serving as a powerful means of communication. Unless someone deliberately conceals their intentions by controlling their facial expressions, we can often accurately discern their true feelings. Our brains naturally pick up on subtle cues in facial expressions, enabling us to form impressions and make judgments. While some individuals may find interpreting facial expressions more challenging than others, acknowledge that we already possess a foundation in reading faces. Throughout our lives, we have subconsciously honed this skill, and with a little effort, we can progress from an intermediate to an expert level.

Besides that, facial expressions can often reveal more about a person's true thoughts and feelings than words alone. Likewise, there are some instances for someone's facial expressions to contradict what they are saying. For instance, imagine your boss is providing detailed instructions to a colleague who appears to be nodding in agreement and affirming their understanding. However, if their wide eyes and fearful facial expressions suggest overwhelming confusion, it becomes evident that they are struggling to process the information. Similarly, when someone tries to hide their romantic interest in you from their friends, subtle cues like prolonged eye contact, quick eyebrow flashes, and joyful facial expressions in your presence may inadvertently betray their true feelings. Our subconscious mind automatically processes facial expressions, often causing us to overlook their significance. Attention to these nonverbal cues can provide valuable insights into the other person's thoughts and feelings.

However, understanding facial expressions goes beyond their use for manipulation or dominance; it involves harnessing their power to enhance communication and connection. Attuning ourselves to someone's facial expressions allows a deeper understanding of their thoughts and emotions, making us more receptive listeners. This awareness facilitates meaningful interactions and conveys our feelings, benefiting our social, romantic, and professional lives while fostering better conversations.

Renowned public speaker Jordan Peterson recognizes the significance of facial expressions, perceiving them as constantly "broadcasting stories." His skill in reading facial expressions engages large audiences and individuals, creating a sense of involvement and intimacy. Peterson's mastery of facial expression interpretation enables him to effectively communicate his ideas with captivation and clarity, transforming his lectures into interactive conversations.

Additionally, attentiveness to facial expressions empowers us to adapt our behavior accordingly. Recognizing negative facial cues enables timely conversation adjustments and the ability to step back when necessary. This awareness allows us to gauge the progress of interaction and identify opportune moments to shift topics or modify our approach, fostering smoother communication and effective navigation of social situations.

In conclusion, developing the ability to read facial expressions offers numerous benefits. For once, it promotes deeper connections, facilitates effective self-expression, and enhances communication skills. By appreciating the importance of facial expressions and actively incorporating this knowledge into your interactions, you can improve personal and professional relationships, leading to more fulfilling and meaningful connections with others.

CHAPTER 2

HOW TO READ FACIAL EXPRESSIONS

W ith a deeper understanding of the science behind facial expressions, we can now explore ways to utilize facial recognition to enhance our social interactions. This chapter will delve into the practical aspects of effortlessly comprehending the emotions conveyed through facial expressions and effectively responding to them. By honing our ability to read and interpret facial cues, we can better navigate social situations and connect more with others.

See the Differences

Improving your ability to read facial expressions requires examining your approach to social interactions and paying attention to the person you are conversing with. Being proficient in reading facial expressions demands your full attention and engagement with the other person. If maintaining focus is challenging, reflect on the possible reasons. Anxiety or intrusive thoughts may hinder concentration during social interactions for some individuals; increasing exposure to social situations could help alleviate this issue. For others, multitasking may disrupt their ability to focus on a conversation. In such cases, ceasing other activities and concentrating solely on the conversation is the solution. Practicing mindfulness exercises can also help train your brain to remain present and grounded in the moment.

Often, the root of inattentiveness in conversations lies in one's conversational objective. Setting our ego aside can be necessary at times. The inability to genuinely listen and anticipate an opening to interject may result in overlooking your conversational partner and their facial expressions. Direct your focus toward the other party to foster a connection with them. By shifting your conversational purpose to focus on the other person, you will experience immediate improvements in your ability to read their facial expressions. *But what are you looking for?*

Monitoring changes in facial expressions during a conversation is necessary. Even if interpreting someone's expression proves difficult, recognizing when it shifts is typically possible. Such changes signal a shift in their emotions regarding the situation. By combining this awareness with understanding context and recent statements, you obtain valuable information to guide the conversation successfully. For instance, imagine expressing a mildly contentious idea, like a political stance, while discussing your perspective. If the other person's facial expression alters, the context implies that your remark may be more controversial than initially thought. Utilizing this insight, you can determine if it is advisable to redirect the conversation away from politics.

Consider a change in facial expression as a useful alert indicating a conversational shift, prompting you to observe the ongoing social interaction. Trust your instincts when it comes to detecting alterations in facial expressions. As discussed in Chapter 1, the human brain, particularly the fusiform face area (FFA), excels at processing and recognizing faces, including subtle nuances in expressions. With practice, you can consciously identify these changes, typically involving eyebrows, eyes, and lips. Adjustments in these areas signify a noteworthy moment in the conversation that warrants attention.

While focusing on others' facial expressions is crucial, being aware of your own is equally important. Familiarize yourself with your eyebrow, eye, and lip movements, as inappropriate expressions, such as contempt, may hinder connection despite saying the right things. On the other hand, appropriate facial expressions demonstrate engagement and interest in the conversation.

In particular, refine your eyebrow flash technique, a brief upward movement of the eyebrows before returning to their original position. This common gesture conveys interest, effectively communicating your attentiveness to the speaker. Psychologist Chris Frith emphasizes the importance of ostensive gestures like eyebrow flashes, asserting that they signal trustworthiness in the sender.

Practice the Art

The human brain possesses millions of years of evolutionary progress, enhancing its capacity to perceive and interpret facial expressions. To consciously enhance this ability, it is important to practice and attentively heed the cues your subconscious mind provides. Engaging in resonance exercises presents an excellent opportunity to refine your recognition of facial expressions.

For the resonance exercise, it is beneficial to have a partner. While a close friend or family member is ideal for alleviating self-consciousness, finding someone dedicated to improving their body language recognition can be mutually advantageous. Collaborating with a like-minded individual allows you to cultivate the habit of working on your facial expression recognition skills while also providing a platform for comparing experiences and insights on this shared journey.

To commence the resonance exercise, do the following:

1. **Request your partner to display various facial expressions corresponding to different emotions**. Allow your partner to choose specific expressions, emphasizing the

importance of natural representations rather than exaggerated or comical gestures.

2. **Consider your facial expression.** If you perceive your partner conveying a positive emotion, strive to mirror it on your face. Conversely, if their expression suggests negativity, endeavor to adopt a complementary negative cue. Further details on this concept will be explored below.

3. **Engage in discussion with your partner regarding the facial expressions employed during the exercise.** Seek their perspective on whether your facial expression appeared genuine and appropriate for the intended emotion. Verify the accuracy of your perception and attentively consider any constructive feedback they may offer.

Through regular engagement in the resonance exercise, you will gradually develop a heightened awareness of facial expressions in everyday conversations, allowing you to become more attuned to your facial expressions. Consistency in practice is key, as we aim to cultivate a habitual thought process concerning facial expressions, making it more natural and effortless in real-life interactions.

When introducing the concept of complementary negative cues within the resonance exercise, it is crucial to emphasize that directly matching a negative facial expression may not always be suitable for a given situation. Due to the strong empathetic nature of human beings relative to other species, mimicking a negative expression can exacerbate the negative emotions experienced by the other person, thereby offering little assistance.

To illustrate this concept, consider a scenario where you are conversing with a friend who shares the news of their cat's recent demise. Their facial expression exudes profound sadness. Responding with an equally sorrowful expression would only intensify their sorrow. Instead, a more appropriate facial expression would convey sympathy, acknowledging and validating their emotions without burdening them. Thus, the complementary negative cue to sadness lies not in mirroring their sadness but in expressing concern or sympathy.

Similarly, in a situation involving anger, such as a confrontation with a colleague displaying furious and aggressive facial expressions, matching their anger with your expression would further escalate the tension, potentially leading to more conflict. The complementary negative cue, in this case, should prioritize de-escalation. Adopting a facial expression of calm concern communicates a non-confrontational stance, signaling your intent to alleviate the situation.

In contrast to negative emotions, responding to a positive facial expression with a matching expression is generally acceptable. When someone displays happiness, reflecting that joy through your facial expression is appropriate. However, avoid facial expressions that do not align with the positive or negative emotions the other person displays. Projecting a happy expression while the other individual is sad will be perceived as inconsiderate and unkind. Similarly, if they exhibit happiness and your expression is one of sadness, it will dampen the mood and hinder the natural progression of positive interaction.

Deliberate Versus Spontaneous Expressions

When endeavoring to discern facial expressions, consider whether the other person's expression is intentional or unplanned.

A **deliberate facial expression** is consciously controlled and purposeful. On the other hand, a **spontaneous facial expression** arises immediately as a response to a feeling or emotion. Psychologists at the Watson Research Center have conducted research revealing that distinct parts of the brain are engaged when producing deliberate or spontaneous facial expressions.

Have you ever observed an actor and felt you could detect their act? This critique stems from the disparity between deliberate and spontaneous facial expressions. If you cannot shake the sense of witnessing an actor consciously portraying emotions, it is likely because their facial expressions appear overly calculated. Naturally, actors' facial expressions are deliberate as they contemplate their character's emotions and strive to portray them accurately. However, a skilled actor can make deliberate expressions appear genuine and unplanned.

As you might anticipate, spontaneous facial expressions reflect an individual's emotional state more authentically. These expressions arise from a genuine feeling and are expressed without any intermediate process of regulating or concealing the emotion. The spontaneous expression represents a pure form of emotional expression and, to some extent, happens involuntarily. Therefore, it is valuable to be able to distinguish between deliberate and spontaneous expressions.

Deliberate Expressions in Everyday Life

When consciously considering what facial expression to utilize, you actively implement deliberate facial expressions. Despite their deliberate nature, these expressions are not inherently deceitful or negative. Instead, they can be employed in a prosocial and positive manner, benefiting all participants in the conversation. For instance, deliberate expressions can convey genuine interest in the other person's perspective. This approach proves especially valuable if you tend to be less naturally expressive, as deliberate expressions counteract any perception of disinterest. Employing a deliberate eyebrow flash or smile can encourage your conversational partner to continue sharing their thoughts while simultaneously validating their emotions and opinions.

Furthermore, deliberate and exaggerated facial expressions can be employed to influence the overall energy of a room. An exaggerated surprised face, for example, can elicit amusement and foster a sense of relaxation among individuals present. Similarly, a grand and exaggerated expression of delight upon someone's entry into a room can create an atmosphere of warmth and acceptance, making them feel genuinely welcomed.

Remember that an "exaggerated" expression does not necessarily equate to falsehood; rather, it signifies a purposeful amplification of the expression's intensity.

Difference Between Deliberate and Spontaneous Expressions

Though it can be difficult, it is possible to tell the difference between deliberate and spontaneous facial expressions. Studies indicate that deliberate expressions can be observed through facial micromovements lasting less than a second. Due to their brief and subtle nature, consciously detecting these movements can be challenging. However, the brain is adapted for this purpose. As a result, trusting your subconscious when determining whether a facial expression is deliberate or spontaneous is often a reliable approach.

If you feel that someone's expressions are deliberate rather than spontaneous, consider the context of their facial expression. Consider whether the other person has a reason to control their expressions deliberately. For example, if you are on either side of a negotiation table, they have a good reason to use deliberate expressions, and your gut instinct is probably right. In addition to the context of the situation, consider what you know about the other person. If they have a reputation for being more guarded, they are less likely to allow themselves spontaneous facial expressions.

As former FBI Agent Jim Clemente notes, there is no one facial expression that gives away whether someone is acting deliberately or deceptively. Instead, Clemente explains that you should be looking out for changes in behavior from how the person normally acts. To tell if someone is using deliberate expressions, establish a norm for their facial expressions and be sensitive to when they deviate from that norm.

For example, many people under interrogation act nervously. This does not mean they are lying because being in an interrogation room is a nerve-wracking experience, even if you are innocent. They may fidget and perform grooming behaviors like touching their hair. However, if, when asked some probing questions, they suddenly stop fidgeting and appear very calm, this is a sign that they are using deliberate expressions. They are attempting to manage your perception of them, and this may be a sign that they are engaged in deception.

To stress the point, the idea is a change in facial expression norms. If someone is often anxious, their facial expressions do not indicate deliberateness or deceit. However, if someone is naturally calm and then suddenly starts acting nervously, this might be a sign that something is amiss in what they are saying. Try to take a holistic approach rather than focusing on one particular "tell" or giveaway.

Again, the key is to look for changes in facial expressions. Just remember to apply your contextual knowledge of the situation to your evaluation. A shift in facial expression might indicate a spontaneous shift if something has happened in the conversation to provoke a different emotion. By contrast, if there is a shift in expression that the conversation does not warrant, they might be engaging in deliberate attempts to control their facial expressions.

CHAPTER 3

TOP TAIL SIGNS

A fter learning to read facial expressions and respond appropriately, dig into the mechanical specifics of each facial expression, describing in detail how each of the big five emotions is expressed on the human face. Recognizing these emotions and responding correctly will improve social skills and ensure positive social interaction.

The Contours and Lines

Facial expressions can reveal much about a person's thoughts and feelings. Some individuals also believe that facial lines, which include wrinkles, are connected to past experiences, traumas, and personality types. Chinese face reading, a practice popularized in the United States by Dr. David Snyder, is based on this idea. The concept proposes that various life experiences and suppressed emotions leave visible lines on the face, enabling those with expertise in this field to gather information about an individual.

For instance, Dr. Snyder asserts that a line extending from the outer corner of the eye down to the cheekbone indicates repressed sadness. A line that extends further downward suggests sorrow, while one that reaches even lower suggests deep grief.

Chinese face reading is closely tied to traditional Chinese medicine, but its scientific validity is not universally recognized. Nonetheless, engaging in Chinese face reading exercises with a friend can be an enjoyable way to enhance one's ability to perceive and interpret facial expressions during everyday conversations.

To practice Chinese face reading techniques, refer to the following list of emotions and their corresponding facial indications:

- **Skepticism:** Parallel lines above the eyebrows
- **Joy:** Upward-curving lines starting from the outer corners of the eyes
- **Sadness:** Downward-curving lines starting from the outer corners of the eyes, with lines that extend past the cheekbone indicating sorrow, and those that reach the jaw suggesting grief
- **Humor:** A vertical line in the center of the bottom lip
- **Bitterness:** Three short vertical lines beneath the lips on either side of the chin
- **Fear:** Vertical contours in the chin
- **Disappointment:** Downward-curving lines starting on either edge of the mouth
- **Over-nurturing:** Three short vertical lines above the lips on either side of the nose
- **Purpose:** Downward diagonal contours on either side of the lower nose
- **Auditory intuition:** Vertical lines on the sides of the face running parallel to the ears
- **Pain:** Three short lines following the shape of the eye, located just below the outer side of the eyes
- **Mania hyperactivity:** Long, upward-curving lines starting from the outer corners of the eyes and stretching past the eyebrows to the forehead
- **Transformation:** A long diagonal line in the forehead
- **Irritation:** Vertical lines between the eyebrows

Even if you harbor skepticism regarding Chinese face reading, observing facial details can effectively train the brain to focus on facial expressions and become more aware of one's facial movements during social interactions.

The Seven Basic Emotions

Chapter 1 introduced the seven fundamental emotions believed to be universally expressed across humanity. To recapitulate, these emotions are the following:

- Happiness
- Sadness
- Fear
- Disgust
- Anger
- Contempt
- Surprise

A particular perspective postulates that all emotions, regardless of complexity, arise from varying combinations and intensities of these seven basic emotions. For instance, jealousy could be a fusion of fear, disgust, and anger.

Recognizing these powerful emotions in daily conversations is crucial as they serve as valuable indicators for appropriate reactions and cues to adjust conversational approaches. Considering this, let us examine each emotion and explore how to identify the associated facial expressions.

While Chapter 1 briefly touched upon detecting the seven basic emotions, this section will delve into greater depth.

Happiness

Recognizing happiness or enjoyment is crucial for building rapport with others. By identifying happiness in someone's facial expressions, it becomes easier to determine their interests and gauge the effectiveness of your conversational approach. To spot happiness, focus on the wrinkles around the eyes, raised cheeks, and lips that curve upward into a smile.

These facial cues can also help determine the authenticity of a smile. A genuine "Duchenne smile" causes the eyes to wrinkle, forming crow's feet, while inauthentic smiles usually do not reach the eyes. When you observe happiness in someone's expression, continue engaging in the current activity or conversation. Remember the discussed topic to facilitate future interactions and maintain a positive atmosphere by mirroring their cheerful expression.

Happiness positively impacts both social and professional relationships. When people enjoy conversing with you, they are more inclined to engage again, fostering deeper connections and making your presence enjoyable. Being well-liked by bosses and colleagues in professional settings can lead to career advancement opportunities and support during challenging projects.

Similarly, in romantic and social situations, happiness plays a vital role. Dates who enjoy talking to you are more likely to seek additional meetings, and acquaintances who feel happy while conversing with you may become friends. Determinating and responding to happiness paves the way for stronger connections and more fulfilling interactions.

Sadness

Sadness, a complex emotion in interpersonal relationships, can signify vulnerability and trust when others display it. Recognizing sadness may indicate that someone trusts you with their intimate feelings. However, consistently causing sadness can result in others avoiding future conversations with you.

The context of the relationship is crucial in determining how to approach sadness. For acquaintances, focusing on positive feelings is essential for building the relationship. In contrast, when friends express sadness, it may signify their willingness to deepen the connection. While it is unnecessary to evoke sadness, encouraging them to share their feelings deliberately can be beneficial, especially if they initiate the topic.

Sad facial expressions typically involve the inner corner of the eyebrows lifting, loose eyelids, and lips pulled down at the corners. To understand these markers, practice making a sad face in the mirror. When observing sadness in someone else, respond with a sympathetic expression rather than mirroring their sadness. A sympathetic face includes raised inner eyebrows, soft eyes, and a gentle, encouraging smile, which validates their emotions and encourages sharing.

In summary, the context of sadness in relationships is vital. Generally, maintaining positivity is crucial in early interactions, as initial feelings can significantly influence one's impression of another person. By understanding the role of sadness in relationships and responding appropriately, you can foster deeper connections and navigate various interpersonal situations effectively.

Fear

When encountering someone displaying fear, discern the cause of their emotion quickly. If you suspect their fear stems from something you said or did, consider altering the conversation or politely excusing yourself to prevent further distress. Fear may trigger a fight or flight response in individuals who feel threatened.

Fearful facial expressions typically involve eyebrows raised and drawn together, upper eyelids lifted, and the mouth stretched open. Responding to fear requires a context-sensitive approach. If the person is afraid of something other than yourself, adopt a calm, reassuring expression similar to a sympathetic face with a slightly wider closed smile. However, if they appear fearful of you, ensure your expression is non-threatening and neutral, especially if you previously exhibited anger or disgust.

In most professional, romantic, and social settings, it is essential to avoid causing fear. A tendency to frighten others can hinder your ability to form meaningful relationships. For example, if a heterosexual man's date feels afraid of him, this indicates inappropriate and predatory behavior that must cease.

Nevertheless, in professional environments, inducing mild fear might be advantageous. Fear is a multifaceted emotion, not solely related to the threat of bodily harm. In negotiations, detecting fear in someone worried about missing out on a deal or not achieving their desired outcome can be beneficial. Recognizing this emotion allows you to apply pressure and gain an advantage strategically.

Understanding and addressing fear appropriately in various contexts allows one to navigate interpersonal interactions more effectively and foster stronger connections.

Disgust

Signs of disgust are rarely an indication that a conversation is going well. Remember that disgust can indicate not only physical aversion but also moral disgust. Therefore, even mild displays of disgust imply that you have made a serious misstep in social interaction. Consider if you have uttered something politically or ethically controversial or committed a faux pas if you discern disgust on someone's countenance.

Typical facial expressions of disgust include a wrinkled nose, eyebrows drawn down toward the nose, an upper lip pulled away from the lower lip, and a loosely hanging bottom lip.

Though disgust is a negative emotion, it does not always mean the conversation is going poorly. For instance, you may bond with someone over a shared sense of something disgusting or ethically disagreeable. In these situations, responding with your facial expression of disgust might be appropriate. However, be cautious when establishing a bond with a new individual based on negative topics. Negative subjects often tend to be more controversial, increasing the likelihood of misunderstandings and missteps. Additionally, remember that people often conflate their initial impression of you with the emotions they experienced during the conversation.

Regardless, attempting to bond over shared feelings of disgust can be risky in professional settings. While establishing common norms can strengthen social connections, this approach is best reserved for individuals you know reasonably well. Remember that first impressions often intertwine with emotions experienced during initial interactions, so eliciting disgust in a stranger could lead to negative associations. With mindfulness of the emotions conveyed and the context in which they arise, one can navigate interpersonal interactions more effectively and foster stronger connections.

Anger

Should you identify someone's facial expression as angry, take a moment to consider the context and determine whether their anger is directed towards you or something else. Keep in mind that anger, like all emotions, varies in intensity. Mild anger may resemble frustration or irritation, serving as a warning sign that the current topic of conversation is becoming heated. This allows one to steer the conversation differently and prevent potential unpleasantness.

Anger manifests on the face through furrowed eyebrows pulling downwards and tightly rolled or inward-held lips. The upper eyelids lift and retract while the lower eyelids pull downwards and backward, widening the field of vision and preparing the body for a potential confrontation.

Similar to disgust, if the other person is angry at someone or something unrelated, responding with your angry expression can signal that you share common social norms. However, be cautious not to amplify irritation or frustration, as this could lead the person to misdirect their anger toward you. Such a situation could sour the relationship and associate you with their irritation. Instead, a safer approach is to adopt a sympathetic expression tinged with a hint of anger in the eyes. As such, it involves slightly pulling up the corners of your lips into a subtle smile while allowing your eyes to appear slightly hardened and narrowed.

Conversely, when the other person is angry with you, carefully consider your complementary negative cue. If you choose not to back down, responding with your angry expression may be appropriate, but remember that this could escalate the argument. On the other hand, if it is more suitable to alleviate the individual, a blend of sympathy and apprehension is recommended. Focus on your lips, drawing inspiration from sympathetic expressions while allowing your eyebrows to lift and come together, accompanied by a rise in your upper eyelids.

In a professional setting, the role of anger heavily relies on the context. Negotiations can become heated, and competitive dynamics may arise in stressful jobs and offices. While matching anger with anger might be perceived as toughness, it could also be seen as unreasonable. Take the time to carefully evaluate the situation and avoid hastily responding in the heat of the moment.

Contempt

Identifying contempt in someone's facial expression can reveal their low opinion of you, which helps determine future interactions with them. Addressing these feelings is particularly important when the individual holds authority in your life, such as a boss or a family member.

Contemptuous expressions are characterized by soft, natural eyes and a one-sided lip curl, resembling a smirk. The appropriate facial response to contempt depends on the context and ranges from mild sadness (to express hurt) to anger. Your expression should establish boundaries and convey that their behavior is unacceptable. An angrier response may lead to a more confrontational situation and potentially escalate negative emotions during the conversation.

In professional environments, monitoring contemptuous expressions can provide insight into the relative status and office dynamics. Observing who displays contempt toward whom can help you navigate the workplace's social intricacies. Based on this information, you can decide whether to conform to established social norms or challenge unfair situations or instances of bullying. Although adhering to social norms is generally safer, there are times when confronting the status quo is necessary.

Surprise

Surprise and interest are intimately connected emotions, as unexpected occurrences often capture our attention and pique our curiosity. In casual conversations, surprise generally elicits positive reactions. Noticing when someone is surprised by your words provides an opportunity to delve deeper into the topic, as their interest is likely piqued, and they are eager to hear more.

A classic surprised facial expression consists of raised eyebrows, an open mouth forming an "o" shape, and elevated eyelids. Responding appropriately to such expressions varies with context. For instance, consider elaborating on the subject or presenting related information if you have mentioned something intriguing. If you share a joke, reciprocate their surprise with a joyful expression. Conversely, if their surprise results from another person's remark, empathize by mirroring their expression.

Moreover, observe the evolution of surprise expressions, as they typically transition to other emotions within seconds. Monitor whether the surprise morphs into happiness or contempt— the former signals interest and intrigue, while the latter may imply shock at someone's incompetence. Observing these changes in real-time offers valuable insights into social dynamics, especially during first dates or in professional settings where swift, decisive judgments are crucial.

To effectively engage with someone expressing surprise, consider the following tips:

- **Maintain eye contact.** This helps build rapport and demonstrates your attentiveness.
- **Use open-ended questions.** Encourage them to share their thoughts and feelings about the surprising topic, fostering a deeper conversation.
- **Be attentive to nonverbal cues.** Apart from facial expressions, pay attention to body language and tone of voice, which can provide additional information about their emotional state.
- **Share personal experiences or anecdotes.** Relating your encounters with similar surprises can create a sense of connection and enhance the conversation.

These strategies can strengthen interpersonal relationships and improve communication skills in various social situations.

CHAPTER 4

EMOTIONAL CONTAGION

....

This chapter delves into the phenomenon of emotional contagion. Scientific findings indicate that emotions are contagious, and comprehending this process is vital for successful communication. By mastering emotional contagion and its practical applications, you can adeptly shape the emotions of those in your vicinity.

What Is Emotional Contagion?

Emotional contagion refers to the phenomenon in which one person's emotions and facial expressions influence the emotions and facial expressions of others. While many of us have experienced emotional contagion at rock concerts, where the crowd's excitement sweeps us up in its energy, this phenomenon occurs in various situations beyond the concert hall.

Imagine arriving home after a tiring day only to find your family happy and smiling. Thanks to emotional contagion, their joyful demeanor and positive behaviors can quickly uplift your mood. Similarly, the opposite holds: if grumpy and irritable individuals surround you, you may soon find your mood more irritable. An example is the morning commute, where one person's honking horn can trigger anger and frustration among other drivers.

According to Professor Hillary Anger Elfenbein, several factors influence the strength and type of emotional contagion. **Social closeness** plays a significant role; the closer your relationship with someone, the more susceptible you are to experiencing emotional contagion from them. Additionally, **membership in a shared group** enhances the likelihood of emotional contagion, while cooperative situations foster emotional contagion more than competitive ones. **Power dynamics** also play a role, with individuals of lesser power being more susceptible to emotional contagion from those in positions of influence.

It is worth noting that emotional contagion can take different forms. While the initial emotion is typically mirrored, there are instances where emotional contagion produces other emotions. For example, if someone expresses anger, emotional contagion may generate feelings of fear, especially when there is a significant power imbalance involved. The specific form of emotional contagion depends on whether the individuals share a "shared vantage point," meaning they have similar perspectives due to contextual, status, and norm-based similarities.

Understanding the intricacies of emotional contagion is crucial when using it to influence others in social interactions. Consider whether you share a shared vantage point with the individuals involved, as this will provide insights into the likelihood and strength of the emotional contagion effect.

At its core, emotional contagion stems from our innate sense of empathy and our natural tendency to mirror one another. The similarity-attraction effect supports the idea that we are more likely to connect with people we perceive as similar to ourselves, and highlighting small similarities can help build rapport. Mirroring facial expressions and body language instinctively taps into this effect, facilitating communication and cooperation. However, given the strong associations between certain body language and emotions, mirroring specific behaviors can influence our emotional states, giving rise to emotional contagion.

The Mechanics of Emotional Contagion

Have you ever noticed how a rumor can get out of control? This is an example of the ripple effect. The ripple effect is the phenomenon by which emotions, information, and rumors increase in potency as they are shared among a group. Because the ripple effect can apply to emotions, it is worth considering it when considering emotional contagion.

The example of the rock concert at the beginning of this chapter demonstrates the ripple effect. If one person at a rock concert is excited, this will have a limited impact on your excitement, particularly if they are strangers. However, if an entire crowd of strangers is standing up and enthusiastically chanting the band's name, it becomes tough to resist being swept up in that wave of emotion. Emotional contagion can become an incredibly powerful tool when the ripple effect takes hold and involves entire crowds of people.

It is simple to think of other examples. It is simple to become overwhelmed by ecstasy and positive feelings at a large faith event because the sheer number of people involved intensifies the emotional contagion of faith. Depending on your perspective, this can be attributed to the Holy Spirit, a psychological phenomenon, or a combination of both. Another instance of the ripple effect is evident in cases of mass panic. You might be able to remain composed if one person is running down the street, screaming in fear, but it becomes much more challenging to maintain a calm demeanor if everyone is running around in a state of terror.

The ripple effect amplifies the power of emotional contagion and underscores the importance of utilizing emotional contagion for prosocial actions. There is a rationale behind the prohibition of yelling "fire" in a crowded theater: the emotional contagion of fear, coupled with the ripple effect, can lead to people getting injured in the resulting panic. On the other hand, emotional contagion and the ripple effect can be harnessed to bring about positive change. Psychologist Sigal G. Barsade discovered that employing emotional contagion to foster positive feelings within a group resulted in "improved cooperation, decreased conflict, and increased perceptions of task performance." Conversely, the opposite effect was observed when emotional contagion propagated negative feelings within a group.

Spreading the Emotions

With all of this in mind, let us consider how you can utilize emotional contagion to influence people positively. We can break down deliberate emotional contagion into four distinct steps:

1. **Be aware of your mood and body language.** To effectively engage in deliberate emotional contagion, you must first comprehend your emotions and facial expressions. Ensure that your expressions align with the desired emotion you intend to convey; otherwise, your influence on others may not be successful. Additionally, consider other body language elements that may support or impede your efforts.

2. **Maintain direct eye contact.** In one-on-one conversations, appropriate eye contact is essential. However, when attempting to influence a group through emotional contagion, establish eye contact with each individual, enhancing their susceptibility to your expressions and reinforcing the contagion's potency.

3. **Counteract negativity.** In a group setting, identify those displaying negative expressions and body language. Engage them in conversation to prevent their negativity from undermining your positive emotional contagion efforts. Alternatively, minimize eye contact with such individuals to avoid absorbing their adverse emotions.

4. **Set suitable behavioral norms.** For emotional contagion to thrive, ensure the environment supports and encourages the expression of intended emotions. For instance, when fostering a cheerful atmosphere, promote an environment conducive to happiness. Conversely, to prevent negative emotions from spreading, contribute to establishing norms that discourage openly expressing certain feelings, such as anger, thereby counteracting potential emotional contagion that could incite irritation among the group.

Additionally, observe others employing these steps, as it could indicate their engagement in deliberate emotional contagion. However, it is important not to resist their efforts automatically. While these techniques may seem somewhat manipulative when broken down like this, remember that someone simply trying to spread positivity is technically engaging in deliberate emotional contagion.

The most effective use of emotional contagion is fostering group cooperation. When everyone feels positive and motivated, the ripple effect contributes to a cycle of positivity. As people experience motivation, emotional contagion is more likely, resulting in a continuous loop. Employing emotional contagion in this manner can enhance productivity in the workplace and cultivate a sense of partnership and collaboration among individuals, which is why effective leaders frequently utilize it.

For instance, consider a scenario where you are working on a challenging group project at the workplace. Perhaps it is late evening, and everyone must return to complete this crucial assignment. If left to unfold naturally, people may feel irritable and demoralized. Fatigue sets in, the desire to go home intensifies, and frustrations mount due to the slow progress. This creates a natural emotional contagion effect, causing negative emotions to spread throughout the group and intensify. Not only does this lead to an unpleasant evening for everyone involved, but it also hampers productivity, slowing down the project and prolonging the time spent in the office.

In contrast, you can prevent this negative scenario by employing deliberate emotional contagion techniques. Purposefully fostering positive emotions within the group can encourage cooperation and expedite completion of the work. This approach allows you to avoid negative interactions with your colleagues, enhance the quality of your work, and earn recognition for your leadership skills in the future.

The Potency of Negative Emotions

Unfortunately, research suggests negative emotions are more easily spread than positive ones. This is probably because of a negative bias hardwired into our brains through evolution. Evolution favors creatures that assume the worst when a nearby bush is rustling because even if it is just the wind nine times out of ten, the pessimistic creature survives when it is a snake. As such, humans have evolved to have a negative bias, such that we pay more attention to potentially threatening situations than positive ones.

This negative bias kept our ancestors alive, but in an age of modern conveniences and safety laws, it is less necessary and has downsides. Emotional contagion represents one of the downsides of our negative bias. Because we attend to expressions of negative emotions more than expressions of positive emotions, emotional contagion is more likely to work on negative emotions.

This brings home the importance of being careful when you can tell someone is in a bad mood. Like with a cold, you can catch irritability. If someone is always in a bad mood, limiting your interactions with them in the name of self-care is okay. This reduces the likelihood of contagion. Alternatively, if you are responsible for a team's performance, you must be aware of negative people to manage how they affect the group. If the individual is persistently a negative influence, it might be worth talking to them to see if there is something you can do to help.

Some unscrupulous individuals may use the potency of negative emotional contagion for their ends. In particular, be wary of attempts to scapegoat or scaremonger. Because negative emotional contagion is relatively easy, fostering suspicion and demonizing a particular individual or group can be straightforward. If this happens, think about how to combat this negative emotional contagion with positive emotional contagion. Moreover, try to distance yourself from people who habitually use emotional contagion in this way. They are toxic and manipulative, and you are better off with them out of your lives.

Emotional Energy

When considering emotional contagion, you will find that the more intense your emotion, the more likely it is to spread. Consequently, you should think about displaying your emotions more intensely when you want to deliberately use emotional contagion techniques.

In Chapter 3, we outlined the seven basic emotions and what they look like when expressed on the face. The intensity of the emotion displayed corresponds to the strength of these facial movements.

For example, let us consider happiness. A happy facial expression involves wrinkles around the eyes, raised cheeks, and pulling the lips from the corners into a smile. You can slightly exaggerate this facial expression to increase the potency of emotional contagion. Bring your lips a little further into a bigger smile, allow that smile to reach and crease your eyes (forming a Duchenne smile), and raise your cheeks further. By consciously exaggerating your facial expression, you will express a greater intensity of happiness that is more likely to spread to the people around you.

It is particularly worth thinking about emotional intensity when trying to influence a group because, in a group setting, people are paying attention to numerous individuals at once. Unlike in a one-on-one setting, where the other person is constantly looking at your face and eyes, everyone must pay attention to everyone else in a group setting. As such, you want your facial expressions to be easily recognizable and attention-grabbing for emotional contagion.

However, when emphasizing your facial expressions, avoid over-doing them. A grotesquely exaggerated happy face can look intensely creepy, as various horror movies have proven. If you are unsure where the line is, consider practicing in the mirror to see your face when you exaggerate a little. Follow your gut: If your facial expression is creepy or disingenuous, do not hesitate to dial it back a little.

On the other hand, if you establish good control over your facial expressions, perfect emotional contagion skills, and read other people's faces, you will be in a great position to build rapport and positively influence others.

Book 2: Gestures and Postures:

Body Language Brilliance —
Unlocking Confidence and Connection
Through Gestures and Postures

Kirsten Rae Evans

TABLE OF CONTENTS

INTRODUCTION

Your posture can have a significant impact on your social interactions. You might be uttering all the appropriate words and employing facial expressions correctly, but you will not appear at ease in the conversation if you are hunched up and defensive. If you do not appear comfortable, your confidence will diminish, and your conversational partner will detect that uneasiness, which may also make them feel unsettled.

This portion of the book delves into gestures and postures, highlighting how to use appropriate body language to enhance your interactions. We will explore power poses and open posture, your walking style, hand gestures, and other intricate details such as proxemics. These aspects of body language play a crucial role in human communication and can significantly impact your prospects for employment, romantic relationships, and the formation of close interpersonal connections.

By adopting a confident posture, you may feel more confident. The brain operates in fascinating ways, and associations work in both directions. If your brain associates a confident posture with feeling confident, not only will your confidence influence your posture, but your posture will also have a reciprocal effect on your confidence.

CHAPTER 1

MOVEMENT TO BOOST CONFIDENCE

....

Throughout this chapter, we investigate how body language impacts personal emotions and promotes a sense of confidence during crucial social engagements. Our focus is primarily on posture and hand gestures, which aim to enhance self-assurance and generate a commanding presence.

Power Pose

Think about your current posture as you read this book. *Are you adopting a high or low power pose?*

There is an extraordinary commonality in posture across humans and the animal world. High-power poses are about expanding your size. Gorillas may expand their shoulders, snakes may draw up to full height, birds may unfurl their wings, and humans may widen their shoulders and stretch their arms. By contrast, low-power poses are about making you smaller. Again, this is seen across a wide variety of species. When it comes to humans, we bunch our shoulders, cross our limbs, and keep our heads down.

Professor Amy Cuddy, a Harvard Business School social psychologist studying nonverbal behavior, notes that we can use our posture to influence our feelings. Adopting a high- or low-power pose for just two minutes can have a measurable effect on the level of certain hormones in the body. To demonstrate the truth of this hypothesis, Professor Cuddy looked at testosterone and cortisol. Testosterone is the main dominant hormone, while cortisol is known as a stress hormone, so high cortisol levels in the system make you more reactive to stress.

In Professor Cuddy's study, she split saliva samples from her participants into two groups. One group would adopt a high-power pose for two minutes, while the other would adopt a low-power pose for the same time. After this, both groups were invited to gamble, and another saliva sample was taken. The results were astonishing. Those in the high-power pose group were significantly more willing to gamble, their testosterone levels increased by an average of 20%, and their cortisol levels decreased by 25%. Meanwhile, those in the low-power group were less willing to gamble, their testosterone levels reduced by 10%, and their cortisol levels increased by 15%.

What this shows is that your posture can have a measurable impact on your ability to handle stress and how powerful and confident you feel. Even if you do not naturally feel convinced, forcing yourself to adopt a high-power pose for just two minutes can influence your hormone levels and make you start to feel more powerful within yourself.

When it comes to applying these findings, think about your posture and the current situation. In almost all contexts, it is appropriate to expand your posture and take up more room, but in many contexts, it is inappropriate to adopt too much of an exaggerated, high-power pose. For example, a classic high-power pose is celebrating with your arms in the air, forming the shape of a "V" above your head. Not always appropriate for social situations!

Conversely, you can use exaggerated high-power poses before a social interaction you know will be challenging or stressful, such as just before a first date or a job interview. Find a private place and practice a big, high-power pose for two minutes. This will boost your confidence and increase your ability to handle the stress of the situation. Psychologists from the University of Bamberg have found that even if this activity does not affect your physiology, it is nonetheless likely to positively affect your self-perception and confidence.

Meanwhile, use less exaggerated, high-power poses to boost your confidence and stress tolerance during other social interactions. The main parts of your body to think about are your arms, shoulders, and neck, especially when you are standing (when sitting, also pay attention to whether your legs are tucked beneath you or bunched together). Low-power poses involve hunching your shoulders, bringing your arms across your body, and bringing your head down toward your chest. Open your posture by widening and rolling back your shoulders, uncrossing your arms, and removing your head from your torso.

Note that this use of power poses is not just about dominance. The main purpose of power poses is to give you more confidence, allowing you to express your personality more effectively. Adopting a non-exaggerated power pose in normal social interactions gives you a more confident and likable presence that others will react to positively.

Finally, in situations where power plays and status competition are relevant, remember that we often respond to high-power poses with low-power poses and vice versa. Suppose you are in a business negotiation. In that case, exaggerate your high-power pose to give yourself the edge over the other person: slightly puffing out your chest, making big hand gestures, and keeping your shoulders nice and wide.

Walking

Many of us are familiar with the "royal walk," the British royal family typifies. The royal walk radiates class, elegance, and confidence, making it an excellent walk to emulate when arriving at social events, meetings, or interviews.

Think of it this way: We all know how important first impressions can be. However, what is the first thing people notice about us when we walk into a room? What we are wearing and how we are walking. As such, it is vital to present yourself with grace and self-assurance.

Tina Leder, a neurolinguistic programming practitioner, gives some great tips on how to perfect your high-status walk. These tips include:

- **Maintain a balanced posture.** Strive for a neutral stance, neither adopting a low-power nor an overly assertive high-power posture. Relax your shoulders and avoid overextending your limbs to prevent appearing tense or awkward. A useful tip from ballet dancers is to envision a string running up your spine and through the top of your head, pulling you into an upright position.
- **Walk intentionally.** Ensure your head and eyes point in your intended direction rather than toward the ground or sky. This conveys a sense of purpose and direction. To maintain proper head positioning, keep the flat bottom of your chin parallel to the ground.
- **Allow space for your arms.** Position your arms at your sides, with hands slightly away from your hips, creating a subtle inverted "V" shape. This stance projects openness and confidence without appearing clumsy.

- **Learn from those with a high-status gait.** Observing and emulating the body language of individuals who exude elegance and grace can be helpful. Take note of their movements, arm positions, and head carriage. Practice incorporating these elements into your walk.

There are different variations of high-status walks. In particular, British male royals often walk with their hands behind their backs, which expands their shoulders and forces their backs to be straight. Though this does not involve keeping your arms spaced, it nonetheless expands your posture without being too much.

In addition to your posture, your walking pace is worth thinking about. If you are walking alongside someone else, you will want to match their pace and take strides to continue speaking to your conversational partner without getting out of breath. Be careful about taking too long a stride in your walk, as this can stretch the leg muscles and result in an awkward-looking gait. Instead, try to keep your hips level and your steps uniform in length.

Consider what your feet are doing with each step when thinking about your pace and gait. When you step, your heel should touch the ground first, not your toes. This aids in balance and thus makes you look more elegant.

With high-status walks, you may find it feels unnatural when you first start practicing. After all, you have been walking in a particular way your entire life, so you can expect it to feel strange if you start amending your gait. Unfortunately, there is no quick fix for this issue. The key is practice. The more you practice your new and improved walk, the more natural it will feel. Keep it up, and keep going until you no longer have to think about how you are using a high-status walk.

Hand Gestures

Aside from our mouths, we communicate more with our hands than any other part of the body. As such, it is vital to use hand gestures correctly. We use our hands for pointing, motioning, showing, and even signing. Hand gestures can radically change the tone of a conversation, transforming it from awkward to pleasant.

The basic thing to think about with your hands is whether your palms are showing. Human beings have evolved to be more trusting of people who show their palms because you cannot hold a weapon and show your palms at the same time. If you want to see this in action, try abruptly hiding your hands behind your back when you talk to someone. You will probably notice them seeming taken aback or suddenly on edge, even though they might not be able to explain why this is the case. This is a trick sometimes used by interrogators who want to wrongfoot a suspect.

Most of the time, however, you do not want to make your conversational partner feel uncomfortable. If you are trying to build rapport or foster a deeper connection with the other person, make sure your palms are visible. This means taking them out of your pockets, keeping them in front of your body rather than behind your back, and using them to gesture. Wide, open gestures supplement a power pose, keeping your posture confident and powerful.

Once you get used to keeping your palms visible, you can start thinking about the particulars. The Westside Toastmasters outline the following common hand gestures and how they can be used in different contexts (n.d.). Let us go through some of these in turn.

Hand Gestures

The following are particular hand gestures:

Rubbing the Palms Together

Rubbing the palms together is a common gesture of positive anticipation. For example, someone being served a lovely meal might rub their palms together.

The speed of the gesture can indicate the sincerity involved. Someone rubbing their palms together quickly is more likely to be genuine, while someone rubbing their palms together more slowly might be more devious.

If you want to emphasize something positive, you might use this hand gesture. For example, if you are trying to sell something to a customer, you might supplement your sales pitch by rubbing your hands together. Similarly, you can use this gesture if you want to indicate to a colleague or friend that you are looking forward to an event.

Meanwhile, it is worth looking out for this hand gesture in others because this can give you useful information about their levels of positive expectation. Again, if you are trying to sell someone something, you will know you are on the right track if the customer rubs their palms together.

Clenched Hands

When someone has their hands clenched, this often communicates that they are in a negative mood. Pay attention to how tightly clenched their hands are. The more clenched the hands, the more negative the mood.

Learning to notice when someone's hands are clenched can be particularly useful because it is often a subconscious gesture that exposes their true feelings. For example, if you see someone smiling at you with their hands clenched, chances are that their smile is not genuine, and they are trying to conceal their negative emotions.

Meanwhile, picking up on someone's negative emotions can help you navigate difficult social interactions. If your boss is sitting at the table with a thin smile and clenched hands, it is worth treading carefully so as not to push them into a confrontation.

In most situations, you will want to avoid using clenched hands yourself. In a negotiation, clenching your hands subtly indicates that you think you are losing ground, which might lead your competitor to push their advantage. More generally, clenched hands can make you look uncomfortable and unconfident, which is associated with worse outcomes in your dating and social life.

Steepled Hands

Steepled hand gestures are those where you keep your palms apart but have your fingertips lightly touch their matching fingertips on the other hand. This forms a triangular, steeple shape with your hands. Steepled hands are associated with confidence and power.

If you want to be persuasive or win the confidence of the person you are speaking with, you might consider using steepled hands. When you talk, keep the steeple vertical and pointing upward, and point the steeple toward your conversational partner when you listen to them. This demonstrates confidence in all elements of the conversation.

Meanwhile, if you notice other people using steepled hands, you can infer that they are feeling confident in the current situation. Because this confidence is linked to status and power, this gesture may be positive or negative. Pay attention to the rest of the individual's body language. If they are using generally negative body language with steepled hands, they may feel confident in rejecting you. By contrast, if their steepled hands are combined with positive body language, this may indicate that they feel comfortable and enjoy talking with you.

Hands Behind Your Back

I have said that you normally want to keep your palms open and visible. This keeps your pose non-threatening and friendly. However, an exception to this rule is when you clasp your hands behind your back. Though you are not showing your palms, and it is a little less friendly, clasping your hands behind your back can also be an expression of confidence and power.

This is because clasping your hands behind your back actually puts you in a vulnerable position. If the situation became violent, your torso would be unprotected and exposed, and your hands would not be immediately available to defend yourself. Of course, in the modern world, we do not normally have to worry about situations turning violent but remember that our processing of hand gestures is evolutionarily hardwired into our brains by our primitive ancestors.

As such, if you adopt a pose that makes you more vulnerable to attack, this communicates that you feel confident that no attack is imminent. It shows you feel comfortable in the current situation and are relaxed. Another advantage of clasping your hands behind your back is that it tends to widen your shoulders, slightly puff out your chest, and straighten your back. This helps you adopt a confident power pose.

When deciding whether to keep your hands behind your back, consider what's more important to the social context. If you want to radiate confidence, authority, and power at the cost of some friendliness, then keeping your hands behind your back may be appropriate. By contrast, if you are looking to foster a more friendly interpersonal connection, it may be better to keep your palms visible and expressive.

Hand Movements During Presentations

Hand gestures are particularly important when presenting to a crowd because they are a great way of keeping your audience engaged. Vanessa Van Edwards found that the most viral TED Talkers used an average of 465 hand gestures during their presentations, while the least popular TED Talkers used only an average of 272 hand gestures (n.d.).

One of the things to keep in mind when using hand gestures is not to go too big. Imagine a rectangle from the top of your chest to the bottom of your waist. Generally, you want to avoid your hand gestures going outside of this rectangle. Otherwise, your hand gestures will seem overly flamboyant and distracting rather than helping you communicate your point.

In addition, if you know you will be giving a presentation, think about your hand gestures ahead of time. Consider the emotional beats of what you are saying and how they can be reinforced with the right gesture. For example, if you are talking about growth, progress, or something uplifting, then a good hand gesture involves moving your open palms upward—as if you were literally lifting something up. By contrast, if you want to close a point and make it definitive, consider the opposite hand gesture and push down the air with your palms.

Finally, try to avoid pointing. Pointing can come across as too direct and a little rude. Instead, consider using your entire hand to direct someone's attention, incorporating your palm into your "point" rather than jabbing your finger in each direction.

CHAPTER 2

CONFIDENT BODY POSTURE

We have talked about how hand gestures and power poses can boost your confidence and express a more powerful presence. However, it is also worth thinking about your posture from the perspective of musculoskeletal health and maintaining an open posture that facilitates positive interaction. In this chapter, then, we will focus on how to maintain an open, healthy posture.

Up Straight

Good posture is good for your back. Researchers from the University of Salzburg found that "poor sitting habits and bad sitting posture are often the cause of musculoskeletal disorders like back pain" (Obermair et al., 2008). This finding has been replicated by researchers from the School of Public Health and Safety in Tehran (Hosseini-Koukamari et al., 2021), bringing home the importance of having a good sitting posture if you have a sedentary job such as working in an office.

However, the importance of good posture is not limited to when we are sitting. It is also important to avoid hunching when you are standing, as this can also lead to back pain and other musculoskeletal disorders.

In addition to the health benefits of a good posture, your posture influences how other people perceive you. If you are hunched over or slouched all the time, you will look unprofessional and childish to others. Furthermore, as we have seen through this part of the book, your posture informs how you think about yourself. If you have good posture, you will feel more confident and ready to take on the world.

Your posture informs how other people see you, and this can have a transformative effect on your own self-perception. Dr. Jordan Peterson puts it best (2017):

> People, including yourself, will start to assume that you are competent and able (or at least they will not immediately conclude the reverse). Emboldened by the positive responses you are now receiving; you will begin to be less anxious. You will then find it easier to pay attention to the subtle social clues that people exchange when they are communicating. Your conversations will flow better, with fewer awkward pauses. This will make you more likely to meet people, interact with them, and impress them. Doing so will not only genuinely increase the probability that good things will happen to you—it will also make those good things feel better when they do happen. (p.37)

What are the elements of good posture? We can break this down into a good sitting posture and a good standing posture, as well as some bad postures to avoid.

A Good Sitting Posture

To maintain a good sitting posture, think about the following four elements:

- Make sure you are sitting fully in your chair, with your buttocks positioned at the back of the chair. This will ensure that your lower back is supported.
- Face forward so that your head is neither looking up nor down.

- Bring your shoulders down and back to avoid feeling hunched. Instead, they should feel relaxed.
- Place the soles of your feet against the floor so that your legs are supported.

A Good Standing Posture

Meanwhile, consider the following five elements when establishing a good standing posture:

- Maintain an equal weight through both your feet, and space your feet slightly so that they are hip distance apart.
- As with a good sitting posture, face directly forward and avoid tilting your head up or down.
- Additionally, bring your shoulders down and back so that they are relaxed and not hunched.
- Allow your hands to hang by your sides.
- Gently pull in your abdomen.

Examples of Bad Postures

When thinking about your posture, try to avoid the following examples of bad posture:

- Slouching when you are sitting.
- Any posture that arches your lower back for an extended period
- Hunching your shoulders

Open Up

We have talked about good posture when it comes to your musculoskeletal health and how this can impact how you are perceived both by yourself and others. Now, let us go into a bit more detail about how your posture affects your social interactions.

When it comes to social interactions, we can distinguish two basic kinds of posture: *open* and *closed* postures. As human beings, we automatically make assumptions about other people based on their postures, such as their levels of confidence, receptivity to talk to us, or relative status.

An open posture, therefore, is more inviting. It indicates that you are receptive to talking and that you are interested in hearing what your conversational partner has to say. By contrast, a closed posture indicates that you are disinterested or uncomfortable. If you are trying to build rapport, then maintaining an open posture is essential.

In the last section, we talked about good posture. To some extent, a good, healthy posture is naturally more open than a bad posture, which will produce back pain. Hunched shoulders, which make the individual appear smaller, are indicative of closed postures. However, there are a few more elements to having an open rather than a closed posture.

Think about what your arms are doing and whether they are in a position that makes you take up less space. For example, if you have your arms crossed, your feet are close together, or your legs are tucked underneath your chair (when sitting), you are taking up less space and making yourself smaller. These elements of body language are indicative of a closed posture that may undermine your attempts to build rapport. In addition, think about whether your limbs and head are facing toward or away from your conversational partner. If they are facing away from the other person, this subtly communicates an unwillingness to deal with them directly and forthrightly, which is again symptomatic of a closed posture.

An open posture, by contrast, involves you taking up a bit more space. Your arms and legs are not crossed, and you are using your hands expressively rather than hiding them in your pockets. You are facing the other person directly and perhaps even leaning a bit toward them. You have opened the chest by rolling your shoulders down and back. This is a much more friendly and engaging posture that will help you make friends and come across as relaxed and confident.

The importance of an open posture is supported scientifically. Researchers from the Haas School of Business at the University of California find that "postural expansiveness makes humans more romantically appealing" (Vacharkulksemsuk et al., 2016). In other words, people with a more open posture are more attractive. The researchers suggest that this is because people with a more open posture seem more confident and dominant, giving the impression of competence and power. Importantly, this research was based on impressions made by strangers, demonstrating that our posture is vital for determining our first impressions and how we are instantly perceived by others.

In addition, the idea that our posture affects our own self-perception and mood is supported by research from the Ferdowsi University of Mashhad (Zabetipour et al., 2015). Adopting a closed posture has a negative impact on our mood, making us feel less confident while adopting an open posture has a positive impact.

Therefore, when thinking about a good posture, also consider whether it is an open posture. Keep your shoulders down and wide and your back straight, but also make sure that your arms are not folded and your legs are uncrossed. This will help you seem confident, relaxed, and receptive to forming new relationships.

Correcting Your Posture

Now that we have considered the basics of a good, open posture, it is worth thinking about how to implement these ideas in your daily life. The trouble is that we often do not think about our posture and fall back into bad habits, especially if we have been sitting or standing with bad posture for some time. The end goal is to have a good posture without thinking about it, but this will require practice and habituation to make a good, open posture your default posture.

In the meantime, we will consider some practical steps to establishing a good posture habit.

Setting Reminders

As you start to form a new posture habit, it will be important to increase your awareness of your posture. This will allow you to notice when you have slumped into a slouch or other closed pose, giving you the opportunity to correct your posture while you are at your desk.

A tried-and-tested way to improve awareness of your posture is to set yourself reminders to think about it. This might take the form of post-it notes on your desk or on the edge of your computer monitor, or it might take the form of timed reminders on your phone. Whenever you notice a reminder and take the time to correct your pose, remember to congratulate yourself for taking steps to improve your posture. You are being diligent and working hard to improve your musculoskeletal and social health.

As time goes on, you may find that your posture is already positive and open when the reminder comes in. This is a great sign that you are forming a new, healthy habit and that good posture is becoming more natural. Reflect on the progress you have made and keep persevering until the reminders become less and less necessary.

Physical Exercises

In addition to setting yourself reminders, you can use physical exercises to improve your flexibility, loosen tightness in your back, and habituate yourself to thinking more about your posture.

Consider practicing yoga or pilates or getting in the habit of performing stretching exercises as part of your daily routine. A quick search on YouTube can find many guided exercises for all competency levels, and these exercises can have a profound impact on your core strength and general flexibility. Remember that the more you use these muscles, the more aware you will be of them. This will further improve your ability to notice and correct bad posture in your daily life.

A particularly simple and effective exercise is the chest opener. This is a great exercise because it encourages an open posture, straightens your back, and rolls your shoulders down and back. The chest opener exercise consists of the following steps:

1. Stand with your back straight and your feet about hip-width apart.
2. Bring your arms behind your back and interlace the fingers of both hands, pressing your palms together. If you do not have the flexibility to do this yet, you can instead grasp a towel behind your back.
3. Think about an invisible line running through your spine, neck, and head. Try to keep this line straight and look directly forward.
4. Inhale deeply as you bring your interlaced hands toward the floor and lift your chest upward.
5. Hold this pose for five deep breaths.
6. After five breaths, relax from the stretch for a few breaths.
7. Repeat these steps at least ten times.

Intermittent Standing

If you work in an office or are otherwise sitting all day, a great way of freeing up your posture and preserving your musculoskeletal health is to occasionally stand and walk about. Dr. Alicia Thorp and her team found that standing up every thirty minutes reduces both levels of fatigue and musculoskeletal discomfort, especially if you are overweight or obese (2014).

Changing your posture regularly not only helps with back pain and other discomforts but also brings attention to your posture. Each time you stand or sit down, think about your posture and whether it is open or closed. Each change in posture is an opportunity to improve your posture and habituate your body to a better posture.

In addition to intermittent standing, you might consider using a standing desk. Standing desks normally give you the option of standing or sitting, but studies suggest that if you have a standing desk, you are more likely to regularly change your posture and stand for longer (Straker et al., 2013). This brings all the benefits of intermittent standing to your posture.

Build a repertoire of familiar postures that you are comfortable adopting. Keep practicing good postures when sitting and stand-ing, and occasionally shift between them so you can teach your body how it feels to consciously adopt a better posture. If you keep up this good habit and maintain your perseverance, you will find yourself more naturally adopting a good, open posture.

Chapter 3

Posture for Effective Communication

....

This chapter brings together some of the lessons from Chapters 5 and 6 and considers real-world applications for some poses and postures. We will look at some specific poses and how they are best utilized, either as a private method of boosting confidence or as a public posture for expressing power and competence. In addition, we will consider how it is sometimes appropriate to drop the power pose and focus on a friendly rather than a powerful posture.

The Stances of Power

We have talked about power poses and how it is important to have an open, friendly stance. In this chapter, we will consider some specific poses in more detail and how you can use them to show confidence and inspire it in others.

The purpose of power poses is twofold. Adopting a pose that your brain associates with confidence will make you feel more confident. This will radiate through your presence and help facilitate positive social interactions, which, of course, will only improve your confidence further. Secondly, adopting a power pose will help other people see you as confident, even if you are not feeling it. They will feel comfortable talking to you, and you will build rapport and respect more easily.

Arms to the Sun

The first power pose we will consider is the arms to the sun pose. It involves stretching your arms out to the sky while keeping your face and palms angled upward. The movement of your arms will naturally lift and open your chest, while your feet should be planted firmly on the ground to give you good balance.

The arms to the sun pose is great for when you need a power pose to boost your own self-confidence. Standing in this pose for one minute or so helps you feel energized and powerful, giving you the confidence you need for an upcoming engagement.

On the other hand, the arms to the sun pose is very dramatic. This means that while it is appropriate for psyching yourself up, it is less appropriate when you are having social interactions. Use the arms to the sun pose in private, just before a first date, giving a presentation, or joining an important meeting.

The LBJ

The LBJ, named in tribute to President Lyndon B. Johnson, is a great power pose to adopt in business situations, as it radiates dominance and power. To adopt the LBJ power pose, you need to be standing up and have a nearby table or chair on which you can rest your hands. You place your hands on that surface, leaning your body slightly toward it. This creates a looming posture that is dominant and a little bit intimidating without going too far.

The LBJ power pose is useful in situations where relative status is important and needs to be carefully managed. You might use the power pose in negotiations or in important meetings or presentations where you need to command the room. However, it is less appropriate in situations that are more informal and friendly. Because the LBJ pose is domineering, it is inappropriate for building rapport or when trying to build a romantic connection.

The Pride Pose

The pride power pose is similar in function to the arms to the sun pose. Think of Usain Bolt has just won the 100m at the Olympics, with his arms held upward and forming a triumphant "V" shape, his head angled upward to the adoring crowds. Your hands can either be open or clenched in determined fists.

There is evidence that the pride pose is a natural expression of pride hardwired into human nature. Even people born with congenital blindness adopt the pride pose when they enjoy success or accomplishment.

Like the arms to the sun pose, the pride pose is not appropriate in everyday situations but can be helpful in psyching yourself up before an important event—or when celebrating a sports victory! Use the pose to help you feel more confident and ready for an important conversation where you need to be at your best.

The Vanna White

Named for the American television personality and co-host of *Wheel of Fortune*, the Vanna White power pose involves wide, open gestures with your arms that are perfect when giving a presentation or addressing large groups of people. To adopt the pose, stand with your feet flat against the floor and allow your arms to sweep expressively as you talk.

The Vanna White pose is a power pose because it involves taking up more space and expanding your posture. Though it can be inappropriate in intimate social interactions, you can use smaller Vanna White poses when presenting in a meeting or giving a talk to a group of people. Any subtle gesture that takes up more space will add to your presence, such as reaching out to the whiteboard you are referring to or gesturing to someone else in the room.

The Wonder Woman

You are probably familiar with the Wonder Woman pose. Stand with your feet apart, lift your chest and head, and place your hands on your hips.

The Wonder Woman power pose is like the arms to the sun and pride poses in that it is best used to boost your confidence before an important social interaction rather than in the social interaction itself. However, a subtler version of the Wonder Woman pose can be used in conversation without looking out of place. You can do this by adopting the pose, but with your head level and your feet not so far apart. This will help you radiate dominance and confidence when having conversations where it is important to make an impression.

The Smile

Though it is not really a power pose, no discussion of confident body language would be complete without mentioning the impact of a big smile. Psychologists have found that the simple act of forcing yourself to smile can boost your mood and your confidence (Marmolejo-Ramos et al., 2020).

An exaggerated, silly smile should be avoided in actual conversations, but it is a great technique for boosting your confidence in private. Meanwhile, genuine smiles are a fantastic method for presenting yourself as confident and friendly, helping you build rapport and make lasting social connections.

The Space Law

A recurring theme in this part of the book is the idea of taking up more space. As noted at the start of Chapter 5, the idea of showing dominance and power by taking up more space is seen across many kinds of species, from birds to primates. Think of a pufferfish puffing itself up to show dominance, a gorilla opening its chest, a peacock expanding its plumage, or even a snake uncoiling and rising upward.

At its heart, the main function of a power pose is to occupy more space. This exerts dominance and mild aggression without being violent. Puff out your chest a bit, allow your arms to take up a bit more room, and adopt a wider stance with your feet. You will be surprised by the difference it makes.

However, as with many elements of body language, it is crucial to exercise moderation. Someone who puffs up their chest too much or stands with their feet too far apart can look like a parody of themselves. Consider opening your stance just a little and taking things from there. Practice your stance in the mirror and judge whether you think it looks unnatural or forced. Remember that even if you struggle with body language, your subconscious brain is evolved to recognize and process all the different ways human beings communicate. As such, if something looks unnatural to you, trust your gut.

Proxemics

When thinking about space, you can also think about your relative distance from the person you are talking to. Generally, we subconsciously move toward people and things we are attracted to and away from people and objects we do not like. Furthermore, physical closeness and emotional intimacy are associated, such that we naturally stand closer to people we know and trust.

Keeping these proxemics in mind, pay attention to how other people stand relative to you. If they are leaning slightly toward you and are standing relatively close, this is a good sign that they like you. This can be particularly useful in judging whether someone is romantically interested in you. If they touch you, such as briefly placing their hand on your arm, even better. By contrast, if they are leaning away from you or standing at a slight distance, this means that they are not open to increasing your levels of intimacy at that moment.

Because intimacy and closeness are so strongly connected, it is very important not to overdo it. Standing inappropriately close to a relative stranger will come across as predatory and creep the other person out. Instead, play things safe and test the waters. If you are speaking with an acquaintance and want to get to know them a little better, try leaning a little toward them and then leaning back to your original position. If they respond with positive body language and do not subconsciously lean back, this suggests that they are also interested in a closer friendship. Meanwhile, if they do lean back, you have tested the waters without crossing any boundaries.

If someone does not reciprocate your gestures, do not take it personally. We all have different boundaries. Just because they are not ready for a more intimate connection now does not mean that they will not feel differently in the future. Maybe they are a little shyer than you or take a little longer to trust. As such, do not take it to heart and test the waters occasionally to see if anything changes in the future.

Drop Your Defenses

We have discussed how taking up more space is a dominant display common to many species. However, it is worth bearing in mind that you do not always want to be engaged in dominance displays. Depending on your conversational goals, you might want to adopt a relaxed posture instead.

As it is, a relaxed posture used correctly can itself be an expression of confidence. The evolutionary underpinnings behind dominant postures are ultimately about intimidation and aggression. Power poses exaggerate your size to show your relative strength and deter others from competing with you. A relaxed pose in the right circumstance can show that you are comfortable in the situation and do not feel the need to compete for status or power. This can express self-confidence in the right context.

When engaged in a conversation, consider what you want to achieve. If you are just looking to build rapport, it may be better to forget the power games and just adopt a friendly, relaxed stance. However, this does not mean adopting a closed or hunched posture. Keep your pose open and receptive so you do not give the impression that you feel uncomfortable or defensive.

Relaxed postures are often more appropriate in one-on-one conversations where there is less need to demonstrate your relative status. If you are hoping to build a connection, remember that you want the other person to enjoy the conversation. This means that you should not be competing with them or attempting to subtly dominate them. By contrast, if you are in an inherently competitive setting, such as a business negotiation and so on, make use of an expansive posture to give you the edge over your rivals.

CHAPTER 4

AID YOUR POSTURE

In this chapter, we will look at some extra tips that can complement your open postures, enabling you to make a great first impression in any context.

Dress to Impress

When thinking about your posture, you should also think about what you are wearing and whether it complements or detracts from your current pose. Remember that when you are working on a more dominant presence, it is important to take up and control more space, so think about clothing that assists in that goal.

The modern suit has its origins in military dress and is designed to complement a powerful, confident posture. The suit provides sharpness to your shoulders, which pairs well with a power pose involving broad shoulders and an open chest. By emphasizing the shoulders, a suit gestures at a triangle body shape, which can also help people with other body types look a little taller. Women can also use formal heels to make themselves taller, taking up more space and thus communicating confidence and dominance.

When it comes to business situations where you want to come across as more relaxed, you might lose the jacket and tie. Without the jacket, your shoulders will not be exaggerated, reducing the effect of a power pose. If you are aiming to build rapport rather than dominate the situation, wearing more relaxed clothes can help you communicate friendliness and receptivity to open conversation. Just remember to keep your posture open.

In non-business situations, it is still worth thinking about the context and what you are trying to convey. If you want to give a good first impression of competence and power, you might favor clothes that accentuate your height and the width of your shoulders. For example, a man on a first date might want to add to their presence with an informal jacket that exaggerates the shoulders, communicating to the date that they are confident and self-assured. By contrast, if you are meeting with an old friend and you just want to build rapport and stress connectedness, you might avoid clothes that exaggerate those features.

In addition to thinking about how your clothes affect your posture, it is also worth bearing in mind whether your dress is appropriate for the context. If you are heading to a formal situation and you are not wearing a suit, your dress may be considered inappropriate. Usually, favor neutral colors like black, dark gray, navy, or brown if the situation is very formal, and wear conservative shoes and makeup. Meanwhile, for less formal business situations, you might want to add a bit more color to what you are wearing.

When trying to gauge the formality of an event, think about when it is taking place, who will be there, and where it is happening. For example, a networking event at a very posh bar is more likely to be formal than an event at a sports bar. If the event is full of people you know, then this suggests that formality might be a little more relaxed, while an event with industry professionals you do not know calls for more formal dress. Finally, if the event is taking place during work hours, favor more formal clothing than you would wear to an event taking place on a Saturday evening.

Position Yourself

How you position yourself in a room or around a table will have an impact on how you are perceived by others.

Let us focus first on where to position yourself at a table. The body language experts Allan and Barbara Pease outline four relative positions between two people at a table and what they communicate, as outlined below (1988):

- **The corner position.** If two people are sitting relatively close to each other at a table and sharing a corner, this indicates that they are likely to be engaged in friendly, casual conversation. Sitting in the same corner allows for good eye contact and makes it easier to notice the gestures and body language being used by the other person. If you are sitting at a table and things seem a little tense, you might find that moving your chair to the corner position can help you de-escalate the situation and put it on a friendlier footing. In addition, you might start in the corner position if your conversational goal is to foster rapport or a friendly connection with the other person at the table.

- **The cooperative position**. This involves two people sitting on the same side of the table next to each other. It is often adopted by two people working on the same task or on the same team. If you want to subtly emphasize cooperation and partnership, you might adopt a cooperative position when you sit down at a table. You might also use the cooperative position as part of a sales tactic. For example, if you are a salesperson, you might adopt the cooperative position alongside the client, opposite the technician. This gives the impression that you are on the client's side, which can be useful for building rapport that might result in a sale. Just be careful to avoid invading the other person's space. A good tip is to arrange for the technician to gesture you to a chair beside the client so that you do not come across as presumptuous yourself.

- **The competitive/defensive position.** In this position, two people are facing each other on either side of the table. In a work environment, the physical barrier of the table emphasizes a competitive atmosphere, so consider whether that is appropriate to the situation. The competitive/defensive position is often used when two people have competing points of view or one side is reprimanding the other. It is useful where relative status is important, and you want to emphasize those relative levels of power.

- **The independent position.** If two people are sitting at opposite corners of the table, this indicates that neither person is looking to interact with the other. For example, if you sit at the same table as a stranger in the canteen or at a library, you might naturally sit in the opposite corner to avoid invading their space and to avoid the presumption of communication. With this in mind, you want to avoid the independent position when you are trying to build a connection with the other person.

When it comes to where you are standing, the main thing to bear in mind is your proxemics. In the previous chapter, we talked about how closeness indicates intimacy and how we tend to subconsciously lean toward people we like and away from people we do not want to connect with. Consider what you are trying to achieve in social interaction and position yourself accordingly.

A good trick to consider is to position your competitors with their backs to the door. Human beings tend to be more on edge when they have their backs to open space because our ancestors' associated open spaces with possible sources of danger. By standing in the middle of the room facing the door, anyone talking to you will naturally have their back to the door, putting them more on edge. Relatedly, if your goal is not to be competitive but cooperative, you want to avoid having your conversational partners back at the door so that they can feel more relaxed and receptive.

Face the Light

In the movies, a character with a shadow across their face is presented as mysterious or sinister. They are literally shady. As a general rule, you want to avoid being perceived in the same way.

To avoid darkness falling across your face, position yourself facing toward the light. If a light is behind you, your head will cast shadows across your face, potentially ruining a first-time interaction. By contrast, if there is light shining on your face, you will be more visible to your conversational partner and avoid this unpleasant association.

A small caveat: Though it is important to avoid shadows across your face, this does not mean that you should blind yourself. If you must cover your eyes or are constantly blinking, this can be just as damaging to a first-time interaction. As such, if the lights are particularly bright, you might want to stand at a slight angle to avoid the light irritating your eyes and ruining your first impression.

Stay Away From Corners

If you are concerned with taking up more space and establishing a more dominant presence, you want to avoid standing in the corners of a room. If you stand in a corner, the walls loom around you and give the impression that you are being swallowed up, diminishing your size and presence. Standing in a corner can also seem defensive because you've positioned yourself in a way that avoids being surrounded or snuck up on. With your size diminished and your presence seeming defensive, other people will assume that you are not confident in the current situation. This is to be avoided.

Think about a game of chess. The knight moves in an "L" shape. If it is in the corner of the chess board, it has very few places to go. By contrast, if the knight is in the center of the chessboard, it can move in many different directions and is a more versatile and powerful piece. Similar considerations apply to real-life situations. Standing in the center of a room demonstrates confidence in your surroundings, takes control of more space, and gives you more options for movement.

For example, suppose you are at a networking event. If you are standing in the corner, you look defensive and uncomfortable, as we have already noted. However, you also have less maneuverability. If someone comes to talk to you, you are trapped in the corner and unable to leave that conversation without awkwardness. This will undermine the purpose of a networking event because you will be unable to meet new people and make new connections. By contrast, if you are in the center of the room, you can easily join and leave conversations and get to know more people in your field. As such, avoid corners and take your place in the center.

Walls, Counters, and Tables

When thinking about other obstacles in a room, similar thoughts apply to those we had about corners. In particular, walls can reduce your freedom of movement and diminish the space that you control. This will undermine power poses and other attempts to enhance your presence, causing you to feel and be perceived as less confident than you might want to be. Consequently, muster your courage and stand in the center of the room, even if it feels little uncomfortable. You will find that your confidence naturally improves just by making the decision to occupy more space, and other people will respond positively to that.

When it comes to counters and tables, bear in mind that the brain associates physical barriers with emotional barriers. The point is like what we have been discussing about proxemics: Closeness indicates intimacy. As such, if there is a barrier between you and the other person, this indicates that there is some barrier in the relationship. This can undermine your efforts to build rapport or establish a new connection, so avoid counters and tables if you can.

Another problem with counters and tables is that they encourage you to lean on them. Leaning on a table tends to cause you to bring your arm across your body or hunch your shoulders, forcing you into a closed, defensive posture. It also takes at least one arm out of the equation, reducing your likelihood of gesturing more openly. Unless you are deliberately using the LBJ power pose—and note that this pose is more appropriate for establishing dominance than for building rapport—avoid anything that you might instinctively lean upon. Instead, keep your body straight, your shoulders wide, and away from any furniture that you do not actively need to use.

A final point to note about walls, tables, and counters is the idea of comparative optics. We instinctively compare the sizes of people and objects in our field of vision as part of our depth perception. If you are standing next to something that is large, then you will seem smaller as a result. This is another good reason to avoid furniture and walls because they will tend to be bigger than you and thus diminish your presence of power and confidence.

Book 3:
Human Actions and
Emotions:

Silent Conversations - The Art and Science
of Reading Actions & Emotions Through
Body Movements

Kirsten Rae Evans

TABLE OF CONTENTS

INTRODUCTION

The third and final part of the book considers human behavior in more detail and how you can understand how someone is feeling from their general body language. We will consider theories behind human behavior, intention, and demeanor and how these aspects are irrecoverably linked with different gestures and body language. In addition, we will apply this knowledge so you are empowered to influence the emotions of the person you are talking to and make sure every social interaction is a success.

When thinking about human behavior, remember that learning to influence people is not in itself sinister or manipulative. What matters is how you use this information. Will you influence others so that they feel better and happier to be around you? Ultimately, learning to be a good conversationalist and learning to positively influence people in conversation involves the same set of skills.

CHAPTER 1

BASICS OF DEMEANOR AND BEHAVIOR

In this chapter, we will introduce the concept of demeanor and how it is underpinned by and connected to various elements, such as behavior, feelings, mood, and affect. In addition, we will consider the virtues of stoicism and how a bit of ancient philosophy can help you regulate your emotions and prevent unfortunate body language.

What is Demeanor?

The demeanor of a person is their outward emotional state. This is typically characterized by behavior: what the person says, what they communicate with their body language, and what they do to act on their emotions.

Let us consider a very simple example. Someone is having a bad day and is in an angry mood. But this does not mean that their demeanor is angry. Though it can be very difficult to conceal your emotions—especially when it comes to body language—it is possible to put on a happy smile, regulate your body language, and seem calm and cheerful when in fact, you are not. In this case, then, the person is angry, but their demeanor is not.

By contrast, if the person's demeanor is angry, this will be represented by their behavior. They might be rougher with objects, throwing them down on the table or making more of a noise. Their demeanor might be evident from their body language, seen on their face as scowl or in their clenched hands. Additionally, their angry demeanor may be expressed through their words. They might be more irritable, snap more easily, and generally have less patience for other people. Here, then, the person both feels angry and has an angry demeanor.

Learning to interpret someone's demeanor is important for successful social interaction. Most of the time, a person's demeanor matches how they are feeling, so someone's demeanor provides lots of information about whether they are receptive to conversation and how best to talk to them. In addition, if you can pick apart someone's demeanor from how they are feeling, you know both what's going on in their head and how they want to present themselves to others. When these two elements do not match up, this can be very instructive about the person's motivations and conversational goals.

To fully understand demeanor, we will consider body language and other behaviors that underpin different kinds of demeanor. In addition, it is important for us to have a good understanding of what we mean by *feeling*, *mood*, and *affect*. These are all aspects of emotions and help give us a better theoretical understanding of human emotion.

Feeling

Feeling refers to the subjective quality that is associated with an emotion. It is distinct from your mood and behaviors and is a bit like any other sense emotion like taste or smell. It is your immediate experience of the emotion.

It is hard to offer a definition of feeling, but it can be easily grasped through examples. All of us are familiar with how happiness feels different from anger. Even if you behave in the exact same way when feeling happy or sad, your internal sensation of the emotions will still differentiate the two scenarios.

Another phrase that means the same thing as the feeling is a *subjective emotion*.

Psychologists offer three different dimensions when classifying feelings, as follows:

- **Pleasantness-unpleasantness:** All feelings fall on a range between very pleasant and very unpleasant. For example, happiness is pleasant, and sadness is unpleasant.
- **Excitement-numbness:** Some feelings excite the person having the emotion (whether positively or negatively), while other feelings feel more numb. For example, anger excites the person feeling it, while sadness can leave people feeling numb.
- **Tenseness-relaxation:** If a feeling is associated with the anticipation of a future event (whether positive or negative), it has a higher level of tension, while feelings based on past events involve a sense of relaxation. For example, excitement has high tension, but grief is a more relaxed emotion. This does not mean that it feels relaxing to be grieving; it just means that grief tends to refer to a past event rather than an anticipation of a future event.

Mood

Unlike feelings, a mood is an emotional state that is extended over time. A feeling can be felt in just one moment—phrases such as a *flash of anger* or *rush of excitement* come to mind—but a mood is a bit more lasting as an emotional state.

For example, if you are in a happy mood, then your emotional state of happiness is extended in time and somewhat durable.

This might be reflected in your behaviors, such that it is a fair guess that someone in a happy mood will generally act in a happy way, but remember that you can still be in a certain mood and behave in a different way. Someone who is in a happy mood may scold someone if they do something irritating, for example. The same thought applies to moods and feelings. If you are in an angry mood, you might nonetheless feel gratitude when your colleague brings you a coffee, even though that feeling of gratitude does not mesh well with your overall bad mood. Someone's mood is a more general state of being.

On the other hand, someone in a particular mood will mostly feel the emotions associated with that mood. Otherwise, it does not make much sense to think of them in that mood at all. For example, if someone claims that they are in a happy mood but they have felt miserable all day, we will struggle to make sense of what they were saying.

Effect

The effect is a more technical term used by psychologists to measure emotions. Someone's effect incorporates both their feelings and mood and is often measured through four key metrics:

- **Intensity:** This refers to the strength behind the emotion. For example, someone who is intensely angry speaks and acts in a different way than someone who is only mildly angry or irritated. You might measure the intensity of someone's emotion by their self-reports—that is, what they say about the strength of their feelings—or by observing their outward behavior.
- **Range:** The range of someone's effect refers to the variety in a person's displayed emotions, both in terms of intensity

and type. For example, if someone seems very happy one moment and then very low the next, they are exhibiting a wide range of effects. This can be a useful diagnostic tool when it comes to emotional or mental disorders.

- **Stability:** A person whose emotions change in a predictable way is said to have a stable effect. For example, if a person's effect becomes sadder when you talk about a sad topic but becomes more positive when you talk about a more positive topic, this is an example of a stable effect. By contrast, if the person's effect is unpredictable based on the flow of conversation, they have an unstable effect.
- **Appropriateness:** Appropriateness refers to the match between someone's effect and their behavior. For example, if someone self-reports that they feel very happy but consistently acts in an angry manner—snapping at people, clenching their fists, and so on—then their effect is low on a scale of appropriateness.

The Cognitive Cycle

We are interested in emotions because they underlie how we feel and everything we do. They influence behavior and thoughts, but they are also influenced by those same aspects of human life. This idea underpins the cognitive cycle, which forms the basis of cognitive behavioral therapy (CBT).

There are four elements to the cognitive cycle, listed below:

- **Emotion:** As we have been discussing above, emotion incorporates your feelings, mood, and affect.
- **Sensation:** Sensation refers to those feelings that are not obviously emotional. For example, you might have the sensation of feeling too hot or hungry.

- **Thought:** When it comes to the cognitive cycle, we focus on thoughts that relate to our appraisal of events or ourselves.
- **Behavior:** As noted above, this incorporates what you say, how you act, and your outward expression of emotions.

The basic idea behind the cognitive cycle is that each of these four aspects has a causal effect on the other aspects. For example, if you feel afraid, this influences your sensations by raising your heart rate or leaving you short of breath. Fear causes fearful thoughts of dread or worry and can lead to fight or flight behavior.

We are all familiar with how emotions can influence thoughts and behavior. The crucial point is that sensations, thoughts, and behaviors can also affect our emotions. If you are constantly thinking self-critical thoughts, then you will feel less confident in yourself. If you force yourself to smile, you will feel a little happier. And if you are hungry, you might feel more irritable or anxious. We have come across some of these ideas throughout the book. For example, one of the main uses of power poses is to imbue you with a sense of confidence. This is an example of your behavior affecting your emotions.

Linking things back to interpersonal skills and successful conversations, it is worth remembering that how you act will both influence and be influenced by your emotions. Successful emotional regulation can prevent you from saying something a little off-color or snapping at someone in a way you will later regret. Meanwhile, paying attention to your own body language will help your emotional regulation because you are able to influence your emotions through your behavior. More generally, regulating your display of feelings and mood will help you control the conversation and the tenor of any social interaction.

A Dash of Stoicism

We have touched on how we might work to regulate our emotions. Acting in a positive and confident way will make it easier to keep your emotions on an even keel. The idea that behavior can have an impact on your emotions is the fundamental idea behind the adage *fake it 'til you make it.*

In addition to thinking about your behavior, you might want to do some work on your thoughts and sensations. The trick is to approach the topic like a scientist: observe and make conclusions based on those observations. If you commonly find it difficult to regulate your emotions before lunch, then it might be that your sensation of hunger is affecting your emotions, and it is worth bringing your lunch hour a little earlier. If you are constantly self-critical in your thoughts, then identify these patterns of thought and consider alternative ways of thinking about yourself. These steps will help boost your self-confidence and improve your emotional regulation.

Furthermore, you might consider the ancient philosophy of stoicism. The basic tenet of stoicism is that you might not be able to control what happens to you, but you *can* control how you react to what happens to you. The thought is that if you can master your emotional reactions to external events, you will be able to achieve purpose and happiness regardless of the curveballs life throws at you.

The trick, of course, is learning how to control how you react to external events. You are used to letting your emotions rule the roost and influence how you think and behave, but now you need to reverse that process. The ancient stoics practiced many exercises to improve their emotional regulation. If you are interested in stoicism, it is worth reading a book dedicated to the topic, but we will briefly outline three of those exercises here:

- **Self-reflection:** The ancient stoics practiced self-reflection every day, analyzing how they acted and how they might have acted better. By applying self-reflection to your life, you can work forthrightly on your foibles and weaknesses and identify negative patterns of emotions, thoughts, and behaviors. Knowledge is power. Once you identify those negative patterns, you can start thinking of ways to disrupt them in the future. A good tip is to conduct self-reflections on paper, such as in a physical journal, as this establishes a good context for thinking about the day and gives you something to look back on and identify trends.

- **Gratitude exercises:** It is easier to weather the vagaries of fate if you are cognizant of all the good things you have in your life. The ancient stoics believed that it is important to recognize things to be grateful for, both to remind you of your purpose and to give you the emotional fortitude to tolerate disasters and other negative events. You can incorporate gratitude exercises into your self-reflections by writing down at least one thing you are grateful for each day.

- **Voluntary hardship:** Sometimes, it is worth proving to yourself that you have strength and fortitude. You can do this with voluntary hardship, such as by adopting intermittent fasting or occasionally sleeping on the floor instead of on a bed. Not only does this demonstrate that you can overcome life's challenges, but voluntary hardship also works well to remind you of things to be grateful for. After spending a night on the floor, you will appreciate your bed even more!

Another advantage of stoicism and self-reflection is that you will bring awareness to your body language and how you act. Think of each conversation a bit like a poker game, where your mood and feelings are your cards. You should know your cards, and you should have control over whether you show them to your conversational partner or not. By being cognizant of your body language, you can communicate more effectively and enjoy better conversational outcomes.

Do not take this analogy too far, however. You do not want to come across as emotionless, so there is no need to practice your poker face. The important thing is to maintain control of your emotions and behaviors. You should express yourself intentionally and with purpose rather than accidentally communicating things you would rather keep to yourself.

Of course, if the other person is being a little looser with their outward displays of emotions, this can be useful information for making sure the conversation goes well. In the next chapter, we will consider this in a bit more detail.

CHAPTER 2

INTENTION AND BEHAVIOR

N ow that we understand human demeanor, it is time to consider human behavior and how we can read other people's intentions and influence how they act. We will think about bad behaviors and what we can do to correct them in ourselves and others without undue confrontation. In addition, we will consider the gap between intention and behavior and how this distinction is important in social interaction.

Human Behavior

In this chapter, we take a more theoretical look at human behavior and consider what the implications are for social interactions. Human behavior is a wide subject and clearly has an impact on daily professional and social life. Becoming an expert on human behavior will give you a big advantage in maneuvering social situations and advancing your career.

However, learning to recognize and process human behavior is only one part of the puzzle. Sometimes, a person's intentions and behavior can diverge. An obvious example is when the person is lying to you. Their behavior says one thing, but their intention is another. Though, it is important to know more about human behavior and to question the intentions that might be behind those behaviors.

What is Behavior?

Behavior is defined as actions that can be observed by others. Of course, this encompasses a wide variety of actions that you or others could take. For example, behavior encompasses what people say, their body language, any exercise they might do, typing on a computer, and so on.

However, there are some actions that cannot be observed by others. For example, when you think about something, there is no possible method by which your thoughts can be directly observed. Of course, your thoughts can be inferred from your behavior, but this does not mean that your thoughts are behaviors in themselves.

When we say that behavior is observable, bear in mind that we do not mean that the action *is* observed. Instead, we mean that it *can*, in principle, be observed. For example, brushing your teeth in the privacy of your own home is still behavior, even if no one is there. If someone were in the room with you, they could observe.

In this book, the behaviors we will focus on are those behaviors that are carried out by an individual toward others. In particular, we will think about body language behavior—a person's gestures, posture, and so on—as well as other actions that directly impact you or the people around you.

When it comes to these kinds of behaviors, we can differentiate good behavior from bad behavior. Bad behavior is antisocial. It is often accompanied by negative emotions and moods and has a deleterious impact on cooperation and building rapport. By contrast, good behavior is prosocial. It is associated with positive emotions and moods and can help foster connection, teamwork, and a more productive, enjoyable atmosphere.

Some elements of bad behavior are obvious. If someone is throwing objects about and yelling at everyone that comes near them, they are behaving badly and in a way that has a significant negative impact on any attempt to work with them. However, other behaviors are a little subtler. It is useful to recognize these behaviors in a timely fashion so that you can either correct your own behavior or set boundaries with the individual exhibiting these bad habits. Some examples of these kinds of behaviors are as follows:

- **Being snide:** You or another person might constantly be putting other people down, making small, nasty comments or ill-intentioned jokes designed to belittle or criticize.
- **Acting superior:** You or another person might be acting contemptuously toward others by ignoring what they have to say, not listening to them, or exhibiting body language that radiates a lack of respect.
- **Gossiping:** Though gossiping does not always have to be negative, it commonly is. You or another person might be gossiping about another person's faults or sharing personal business that should not be aired in a professional setting.
- **Over-correcting:** Characterized by the phrase "um, *actually...*" constantly correcting other people over minor errors tends to be unhelpful. Often, people who overcorrect are insecure about their own intelligence or feel the need to boast about how smart they are to others.

Though it can be difficult, it is important to challenge this behavior when it starts rather than later. It is better to seem like you are being a little oversensitive now than to suffer weeks of abuse later.

The first step is to recognize when other people are exhibiting these kinds of behaviors. If something feels off, do not gaslight yourself. Instead, take your feelings at face value and examine the situation for a greater understanding. Try to understand the contexts in which bad behavior occurs and whether you have control over elements of that context.

For example, you might find that two of your colleagues are perfectly pleasant when you speak to them one-on-one but can become snide when they are together. Perhaps they egg each other on in a way that is unpleasant, or they are implicitly competing with one another. To avoid being subjected to this bad behavior in the future, you can take steps to avoid speaking to them together whenever possible.

Some bad behaviors can be corrected simply by avoiding the contexts in which they occur, but others need a more confrontational approach. This does not mean that you need to get into a furious argument with the other person, but you can use body language to demonstrate that you feel uncomfortable with their behavior. Consider abruptly changing your body language in response to bad behavior, such as crossing your arms, taking a step back, or making a frown. This signals to the other person that they are behaving badly without making a scene and gives them an opportunity to apologize or correct their behavior. You will set clear boundaries without having to argue or damage your relationship further.

However, some people will persist in their bad behavior even when you set clear boundaries with your body language. For these individuals, it may be necessary to challenge their behavior more explicitly. An excellent strategy is to question what they just said. For example, if someone has just been rude to you, asking them, "What did you mean by that?" will bring their attention to their bad behavior and make it clear that you will not tolerate their rudeness. If their bad behavior persists, meanwhile, a frank conversation with them in private about how their actions are making you feel uncomfortable is more than justified.

Of course, not all behavior is bad, and you will often come across good behavior in your professional and social life. Your colleague may bring you a coffee without needing to be asked or offer help when it looks like you are struggling. Try to keep an eye out for the little things the people in your life do that you appreciate. Just as it is important to challenge bad behavior, it is also important to encourage good behavior.

The best way to encourage good behavior is to demonstrate gratitude. There is nothing worse than doing something nice for someone and having it go unappreciated. Think of it this way: You would probably stop getting your colleague a cup of coffee if they did not even say thank you. Try to acknowledge good behavior wherever possible and express appreciation. You do not need to gush over them—this can be counterproductive if you make them feel uncomfortable—but a genuine smile, or just a "thank you," can go a long way to encouraging good behavior in the future.

That said, do not be afraid to tell people how much you appreciate them. You do not want to launch into a pre-prepared speech about your colleague's virtue every time they get you a coffee. However, finding time to tell them how much you appreciate the little things they do to make your day better can be an effective way of encouraging that behavior in the future.

Your Own Behavior

In addition to correcting bad behavior and encouraging good behavior in others, it is also vital to make sure you are acting in a prosocial way.

Bad behavior is often a sign of insecurity, especially the list of subtle bad behaviors that we considered above. You may feel that being snide or acting superior establishes yourself as dominant and powerful, but in reality, you just come across as desperate to prove that you are better than everyone else. People who are powerful and competent do not need to constantly remind everyone else that they are. As such, do not engage in bad behaviors that put other people down. Consider what insecurities might be behind your behaviors, and work on those issues with courage and forthrightness. Not only will you be more likable, providing you with more opportunities in your career and social life, but you will also improve your emotional regulation and general well-being.

Correcting your own bad behavior takes courage and radical self-honesty. Furthermore, it is often a work in progress. If your bad behavior has become habitual, you will have to persevere to correct that behavior and be constantly vigilant to catch yourself slipping. However, when your life improves, you will find that the hard work is worth it.

Intentions

Though good and bad behavior needs to be acknowledged and acted upon, bear in mind that someone's behavior does not always match their intentions. Applying a little bit of scrutiny to other people can help you avoid being wrong-footed or deceived by individuals attempting to manipulate you.

What Are Intentions?

A person's intention is their aim or purpose in a particular context. For example, if you are hoping to become friendlier with a colleague, then your intention is to build rapport and foster a deeper connection. If you are trying to sell a product to a client, then your intention is to convince them to make a purchase.

As human beings, we all tend to have similar wants and needs. This results in commonality in our intentions. Some common intentions include:

- To feel more connected to a person
- To feel safe and secure in our position
- To acquire more resources or responsibilities
- To improve our social status
- To feel successful
- To seduce someone

Of course, these common intentions are interrelated. Sometimes we intend to improve our social status so that we can feel more safe and secure.

These common intentions are all linked to our evolutionary underpinnings. We are hardwired to be motivated by resource acquisition and sexual success because these intentions improve our chances of survival and reproduction. Human beings have been highly successful at these evolutionary goals because of our cooperation, so evolution has also hardwired the basic need for social connection in our lives.

Wherever you can, try to understand your conversational partner's intentions. Not only will this inform you of how to act in that conversation, but you will also improve your empathy toward the individual and understand where they are coming from. Always consider the context of your conversation and what their intentions may be.

For example, suppose that you are on unfriendly terms with a colleague, but they suddenly act nice toward you, offering compliments and exhibiting positive body language. Given the context of your relationship, you might naturally suspect that their intention is to get something from you. Meanwhile, if you are on friendly terms with an acquaintance and they invite you for some drinks after work, you might take their intention at face value and assume that they want to foster a deeper connection with you.

As such, think about the context of your relationship and whether the person's current behavior is coherent with their behavior in the past. If there is a notable difference, consider why that might be. True intentions are easiest to infer when there is this dramatic mismatch in behavior.

In addition, think about the context of the current conversation. What has happened recently? Are the two of you in competition, or are you on the same team? Learn to ask yourself these questions so that you can intuit someone's intentions more effectively.

Showing Your Own Intentions

Meanwhile, it is important to think about your own intentions and communicate them effectively.

The first step is to understand your intentions. Often, we act on autopilot and then post-rationalize how we act. This is an inefficient way of achieving our goals. Instead, get into the habit of acting in a purposeful manner. Understand what your intention is at the start of a conversation so you can behave in a way that is consistent with your goals. For example, if your intention is to foster a better rapport with your colleague, being cognizant of this intention will focus your mind on the other person's conversational needs. Meanwhile, if your intention is to sell a product to a client, focusing on that purpose will mean you are less likely to be distracted from your sales pitch.

Once you have determined what your intention is, you should now consider whether to conceal or show that intention to your conversational partner. Do not always assume that it is best to conceal your intentions. Being explicit with your intention is a great way of building trust and thus fostering a deeper connection, though this is dependent on your intention being compatible with the other person's wants and needs. For example, if you are hoping to get to know someone a little better, there is nothing wrong with being explicit and telling them, "I want to know you a little better! Tell me more about…."

When thinking about your own intentions, remember to support them with the appropriate body language. If your intention is to build rapport and you are comfortable being explicit with that intention, then make sure your body language is open and receptive to social connection. Always consider if your body language is appropriate for your conversational goals, and amend your body language if there is a mismatch. Otherwise, the other person will be confused, undermining attempts to build rapport.

The Gap Between Intentions and Behavior

As we have noted, sometimes there is a gap between someone's intentions and their behavior.

In the last section, we talked about the context of your relationship and conversation and whether there is any mismatch between their current behavior and past behavior. These contextual cues can be very helpful in allowing you to intuit someone's true intentions, so try not to overlook them.

In addition, pay close attention to someone's body language. We will talk about this topic in more detail in the next chapter, but people think less about their body language than about what they say. This means that you can sometimes pick up on a mismatch between what they say and their body language. In this scenario, their body language is a truer expression of their intentions.

For example, suppose that your colleague is congratulating you on a job well done, but their hands are clenched. This might indicate that they are unhappy with your success and that they consider you to be their competition in the workplace.

Another example might be in a sales scenario. If the customer is claiming that the price is too high, but they are leaning forward in their seat, this might indicate that they really want the product— even at the current price—and are just trying to save themselves a bit of money.

As such, always pay attention to someone's body language and apply gentle scrutiny to every conversation. You do not need to be paranoid, but always consider the context and whether someone's intention might diverge from their behavior.

CHAPTER 3

EXTRACTING DEMEANOR FROM BODY LANGUAGE

I n this chapter, we build on our understanding of mannerisms, behavior, and attitude and how they are commonly reflected through body language.

Mannerism, Behavior, and Attitude

We have spoken about how body language is an important clue to someone's demeanor, especially because people rarely pay close attention to their own body language. This means that their body language is subconscious and indicative of their real feelings in a conversation.

In particular, we will look at what the other person is doing with their head and feet. The position of the head and the direction of the feet can be very instructive, so it is useful to understand what these pieces of body language mean and when to look out for them.

As with all body language, it is important to remember that these tips are rules of thumb. Always apply your common sense and combine what their body language is telling you with what you know about the person and the situation. For example, though the position of the head is often a useful clue to what someone is thinking, sometimes it is also indicative of pain in their neck. Do not rely on one body language cue to the exclusion of everything else.

Head

We move our heads all the time, but we rarely give it much attention. The direction our heads are facing can say a lot about our demeanor and what we are feeling at any given moment.

We will consider three basic positions for the head and face: downward, lifted, and side-facing.

Downward

A downward-facing head brings the chin closer to the chest and makes it harder to maintain eye contact. It contributes to a generally closed posture and indicates disinterest and non-receptivity in your conversation.

For example, suppose you are pitching your new idea to your boss. They smile vaguely and nod, but their head is tilted downward, and they are not making much eye contact with you as a result. In fact, they seem to be distracted, looking at other things on the ground. This suggests that your pitch is unfortunately not going down too well. Your boss is not interested in what you are saying.

Because a downward-facing head is associated with disinterest, always be mindful of whether there are contextual factors that might prompt the other person to look downward. For example, if they are carrying papers and reading from them when you start a conversation, their head is already facing down at those papers. This will make them distracted and less interested in what you have to say. With this in mind, if you have something important to pitch, wait for a time when they are not already looking downward so your pitch has the best chance of success.

Lifted

By a lifted posture, I do not mean that they are looking up into the air with their neck arched back. This tends to be associated with daydreaming and distractibility because it is hard to look at you and make eye contact when you are staring up at the sky. Instead, by a lifted position, I mean a slight tilt in the chin. Their face will be angled a little upward while still allowing for plenty of eye contact. This lifted posture is a good sign in a conversation, as it indicates excitement and attentiveness.

Suppose you are telling your work colleague about your weekend. You are just making small talk as you log onto your computers, and you are not really expecting them to be paying rapt attention. However, when you mention a particular aspect of your weekend—maybe you went fishing or went up to your cabin—your colleague suddenly perks up. They look up from what they are doing, tilting up their head and chin, and maybe complement the gesture with an eyebrow flash or smile. This body language indicates that you have found a topic that really interests them and that they are receptive to talking more about it.

When you are trying to build rapport, it is important to look out for a lifted head position. If you are meeting someone for the first time or otherwise do not know them very well, conversations tend to be fishing expeditions. You are trying to find a topic of conversation that they will be interested in, enabling further conversation. If you are in this kind of scenario, then you should be looking out for a lifted head position because this indicates that you have found a topic that they are interested in. With this information, you can ask follow-up questions on the topic or otherwise encourage them to talk about the matter.

Of course, the lifted head position is important even outside of conversations designed to build rapport. If you are telling someone something important and they lift their head, this shows that they are engaged and listening to you. If they do not change the position of their head, this might indicate that they are not really paying attention, and you can act accordingly.

Side-Facing

In a side-facing head position, the individual's chin angles up and either to the right or left, putting their entire head at a slight angle. The side-facing head position is indicative of skepticism and possible disagreement and is often complemented with a slight bunching of the eyebrows.

Depending on the situation, a side-facing position may be positive or negative. After all, it is hard to be skeptical of what someone is saying without paying attention, so a side-facing countenance shows that they are least engaged with what you are saying. Meanwhile, if you are talking about a topic where you are inviting feedback and possible discussion, there might be nothing wrong with them expressing a different point of view than your own. In this context, a side-facing countenance might signal disagreement, but it also shows that they are engaged and about to share their own opinion of the matter.

On the other hand, sometimes, you do not want to be met with skepticism. If you are sharing a personal experience and the other person's head adopts a side-facing countenance, this might indicate that they are skeptical of what you are saying. This can be hurtful, but rather than taking offense, it is better to change the conversation to safer ground.

A side-facing countenance is something to look out for when pitching or selling to a client. If you are trying to convince someone of something and their head moves to a side-facing position, this suggests that they are not convinced by your current line of persuasion. Based on this information, you have two options: find another way to persuade them or double down and try to power through the skepticism they are demonstrating.

Feet

As discussed in Chapter 3, as humans, we tend to associate physical proximity with social closeness. We stand closer to people we like and intuitively lean away from people we are not receptive to getting to know. Similarly, the position of our feet can indicate our level of interest in the other person and the current conversation.

When paying attention to your conversational partner's feet, the basic idea is to notice which way their feet are pointed. Generally, people point their feet in the direction they want to go. Combined with the idea that proximity and closeness are associated, this can be very instructive as a body language cue.

Pay attention to whether the other person's feet are pointed toward you or slightly away from you. If they are pointed toward you, this might indicate that they are interested in what you have to say and want to get to know you a little better. By contrast, if they are slightly turned away from you, this suggests that they are not interested in the current conversation. In this kind of situation, you might want to change the topic or ask them a question to get them to talk instead of you.

Meanwhile, if their feet are pointed toward the door, this suggests that they want to leave. Do not take this personally. There are many reasons why someone might want to leave a conversation. They might need to visit the restroom or realize they are running late for another appointment. In this kind of situation, then, the best strategy is to provide opportunities for the other person to gracefully end the conversation without awkwardness.

You can catch up again in the future without your relationship having soured.

Suppose that you are at a networking event, and you've just met another professional in your field. You think that the conversation is going well, but you want to pay attention to their body language to confirm that this is the case. You glance down at their feet and find that they are pointed directly at you. This indicates that your instinct was right. The conversation is going well, and you may have just made a new friend.

Obviously, when paying attention to someone's foot position, try not to stare. A glance should be sufficient to establish the direction someone's feet are pointing. In conversation, you want to maintain good eye contact. Also, if you stare at someone's feet, they might get the impression that there is something on their shoe!

Understand the Other Person

When paying attention to body language, your goal should be to understand where the other person is coming from. Think of yourself as a journalist or a scientist. You are constructing a theory of that person, through which you can gain a better understanding and empathy for what makes them tick. As your theory grows, you will know what kinds of topics to avoid and what kinds of topics will excite their interest, as well as common body language behaviors that reliably indicate their current mood.

Of course, there is no point in having a theoretical understanding of body language if you cannot put it into practice in real-time. The key, then, is to practice and make a habit of using your body language perception skills as much as possible. You want to practice in low-stakes situations so that you are ready for high-stakes situations.

A good activity is to self-reflect on conversations you have with a colleague over the course of the day. After each conversation, try to pick out three different emotions that you intuited from your colleague. For each emotion that you intuited, think about what body language the other person used to indicate that emotion. For example, you might identify that your colleague was engaged and interested and identify an eyebrow flash as the behavioral cue.

When you have identified each emotion and accompanying body language cue, now think about how that emotion impacted the flow of the conversation. Think about how the tenor of the conversation changed: whether it was a positive or negative interaction, whether they spoke more or their tone changed, and so on. Start to build a theory of how their emotions connect with their body language and how their emotions and body language connect to the flow of conversation. Once this theory starts taking shape, you might add to it by paying attention to your impact on your colleague's emotions and what you did to influence their behavior.

If this exercise goes well, you might end up with a fair amount of information about the other person. As such, it might be useful to write down your findings in a physical journal so you can refer to what you've learned about the other person. Just do not share your findings with the person directly. This can give them the wrong idea!

Control the Energy of the Environment

Different emotions tend to lend different energies to a conversation or interaction. For example, if two people are having fun talking about a certain topic, the energy in the room might be enthusiastic and lively. By contrast, if two individuals are sharing sad stories, the energy of the room might be depressive and slower-paced.

We will talk in a bit more detail about how to evoke emotions in the next chapter, but in the meantime, the important thing is to show intentionality. Really think about how your actions and words influence the energy of a conversation, and experiment a little with how you can influence the energy of an interaction. As you practice, you might find it easier to influence a conversation toward more fun and positive energy.

As you get better at controlling the energy of the environment, you will be able to form connections more easily. For example, if the energy of a room is friendly and relaxed, it will be easier for you to build rapport with people you do not know very well. By contrast, if you are trying to demonstrate competence and authority, you might influence the energy of the room to create a more formal atmosphere. The sky's the limit, so keep practicing and see what you can do.

CHAPTER 4

EVOKING EMOTIONS AND INFLUENCING BEHAVIOR

W̓e now have a good understanding of human behavior and the body language that accompanies certain intentions and emotions. We have talked about how this information can be utilized in social interaction, and in this chapter, we go one step further: talking about how we can evoke specific emotions and persuade other people to our way of thinking.

Evoking Emotions

In our discussion of human behavior and emotion, we have focused on how to best intuit other people's emotions from their body language and demeanor. Perfecting this intuition gives you influence over your conversations because you can amend your conversational style in real-time in response to the other person's demeanor. For example, if they are presenting a negative demeanor, you can shift the topic of conversation, while if they are presenting a positive demeanor, you know that your current strategy is working well.

However, in this chapter, we think about other ways of influencing a conversation that is more proactive. Knowledge and empathy are fundamentally important, but they are ultimately reactive.

In my other book, we discussed the topic of emotional contagion and how you can use emotional contagion to affect the energy of a room. For emotional contagion to work effectively, you need to effectively display the body language associated with the emotion you want to spread. This is where some of the ideas for this part of the book come in. If you want people to be engaged and receptive to what you are saying, then inculcate the right emotion by presenting it yourself. Cast your head in a tilted position, and make sure your feet are not pointed toward the door or away from the person you are trying to keep interested.

You will want to evoke positive emotions when you are presenting an idea to other individuals. Emotion plays a powerful role in our decision-making process—we will come back to this idea below—and, as such, someone feeling positive about your presentation can make them act more positively toward your idea. Studies confirm that people are more likely to be helpful and supportive if they are in a good mood (Isen, 1999).

When presenting and evoking emotions, it is okay to be a little larger than life. Really inject your voice and gestures with passion, but make sure you do not lapse into parody. If you are not sure where the balance lies, consider testing the waters and experimenting with different presentations. Once you get the balance right, you will be able to evoke passion and excitement for your ideas in your audience, setting you up for immediate success.

In some cases, you might even want to evoke negative emotions. In my other book, we talked about negative bias and how humans are hardwired by evolution to attend more closely to negative stimuli. One of the effects of this negative bias is that negative emotions can be powerful motivators for action. Consequently, if you can evoke negative emotions against bad ideas, you will be more effective at making sure that those bad ideas are soundly rejected by your audience and colleagues.

On the other hand, it is worth exhibiting a little bit of care. Human beings are naturally tribal and receptive to seeing the "other" as something to be hated or afraid of. This can result in some particularly nasty behavior, so make sure that you are not evoking negative emotions against people but instead against bad ideas. For example, consider the problem of global warming. Evoking people's fears toward catastrophic climate change can be an effective way of mobilizing people to take positive action to prevent it. Because no individual is demonized by evoking these negative emotions, it is appropriate to use evocation in this example.

If you are tempted to evoke negative emotions against other people, please consider this an injunction to reconsider. Putting aside the moral evil of deliberately harming others, it simply is not a good long-term strategy. In time, people will recognize what you are doing, and you will pay a heavy social price for mere short-term advantages.

Decide Emotionally and Justify With Logic

As humans, we tend to make our decisions based on emotion and then post-rationalize them after the fact. There is even evidence to suggest that we simply cannot make decisions without emotions. The neurologist António Damásio discovered that patients with damage to parts of the brain that process emotions (specifically, damage to part of the prefrontal cortex) are often critically impaired when faced with everyday decisions (1994). Think of it this way: Without emotion, we would never be motivated to do anything. A purely logical being might be able to compute and reason perfectly, but without an emotional reason to start working on a problem, they would simply sit in inactivity.

The primacy of emotion in decision-making has implications for how you sell your ideas to others. It brings home the importance of evoking emotions when presenting your opinions. You might give an accomplished, rational argument for your position, but if your audience is bored or put in a bad mood by your presentation, they might still be unreceptive to your views. By contrast, even a bad idea can be effectively sold by a skillful evocation of positive emotions in your audience, as evidenced by the successes of hustlers and confidence tricksters.

With this in mind, the first thing you should think about when presenting your case to other people should be the emotions you are evoking, not the arguments that justify your position. It may seem counterintuitive, but many smart people fail to have the influence they should because they focus too much on logic and not enough on emotions. To avoid falling into the same trap, plan your presentation around emotional beats rather than logical arguments, and do not neglect the emotional state of your audience. This is not to say that you should throw logic out the window, but only that you should prioritize emotions first when trying to convince others. In particular, if you are in a leadership role, focus on evoking positive emotions before implementing any strategy for your team.

Also, bear in mind that no matter what you think, you are just as susceptible to emotional decision-making as anyone else. We are very good at post-rationalizing because we acted the way we did, and the truth is that almost any action can be justified by some flimsy logic after the fact. As such, it is always worth paying close attention to the efforts of other people to evoke emotions in you. This will help you understand their true intentions and allow you to make better decisions for your own reasons.

Attach the Emotion

When putting together these ideas, always think about the intended emotion behind every interaction. Think about your conversational purpose and consider what emotion should be attached to that purpose. For example, if you are hoping to build rapport, then the associated emotions should be eagerness, interest, and cheerfulness. Meanwhile, if you are trying to sell a product to a client, the associated emotions should be excitement and perhaps the fear of missing out.

Keeping in mind the appropriate emotions that underpin your conversational intention can help you express that emotion more effectively. If you are not naturally an expressive or emotional person, then it is useful to have an intentional approach to your emotions so you can communicate better with others. This can make the difference between a successful and unsuccessful conversation. If you are trying to build rapport but sound bored and standoffish, you are unlikely to succeed, even if you say all the right things.

By thinking about the appropriate emotion for your conversational intention, you can express that emotion from the beginning of a social encounter. For example, if you are presenting an idea to your colleagues, thinking about your emotions ahead of time can ensure that you inject passion and enthusiasm into your voice from the very beginning of your presentation. This will increase the likelihood of emotional contagion and a successful presentation.

There is also the element of faking it until you make it. With intentional emotions, you can work on making sure you are presenting the correct body language. Because of the close association between body language and emotion, you may find that you feel the appropriate emotion more genuinely just by acting the part. In turn, this will improve your ability to evoke that emotion in others. People respond positively to authenticity.

Reframe Yourself

When you attempt to evoke emotions in others, sometimes you will be successful, and sometimes you will not be successful. Using the tips contained in this book, you should become adept at intuiting what other people are thinking and be able to read someone's demeanor from their face and body language.

As we noted at the start of this chapter, knowledge of people's emotional states can be helpful when influencing them in conversation. However, this knowledge is useless unless it is acted on. You need to get used to being adaptable in conversations so that you can make use of nonverbal cues in real-time.

To return to a familiar example, this might involve a change of tack or topic of conversation. If you are talking about a topic and the other person is presenting uninterested body language, then you will want to change the topic by asking them a question that gets them talking instead of you.

However, this versatility is not just about what you say. It is also about how you act. If someone is presenting defensive body language, you will want to start adopting a more relaxed, friendly posture to help them come out of their shell. Similarly, if you sense from someone's body language that they are trusting you with important information, you will want to amend your body language to demonstrate that you are listening to them and receptive to what they have to say.

Of course, this all depends on mastery over your own body language. To remain versatile enough to reframe yourself now, you must be able to read body language from others, process that information, and amend your own body language accordingly. It is tricky, and it will not all come at once, but keep practicing. The more you practice, the better you will get at it.

Influencing Behavior

When you influence someone's emotions, you influence their behavior. It is as simple as that.

We have discussed how people make their decisions primarily on an emotional basis. More generally, remember that emotion is the reason for all behavior. A mathematical genius still needs the motivation to solve a mathematical puzzle, and this motivation is ultimately emotional. If they are unenthusiastic or bored by a particular puzzle, they are unlikely to solve it. Meanwhile, if they are engaged or excited by the problem, they will apply all their intellect to the issue.

Because emotion underpins all behavior, it follows that learning to evoke and influence emotions is an effective way of influencing how someone behaves. In the workplace, you will find that when your colleagues are in a good mood, they will be friendlier toward you and more helpful when you need some assistance. They will also be more receptive to your ideas, empowering you to seize career opportunities when they arise.

Just remember that influencing emotion is a skill, and, like any skill, it only gets better with practice. You would not expect to become a concert pianist just by reading a book on piano theory. The same thought applies here. You have the theory in hand, but now you need to apply that theory to the real world.

CONCLUSION

A t the end of this 3-in-1 book, let us consider some key takeaways and what you can do to master your interpersonal skills.

Human beings are inherently emotional creatures. We build bonds based on emotions and are sensitive to the emotions of others through empathy and emotional contagion. We make decisions based on emotions and rationalize them with logic after we have acted. Moreover, we are constantly broadcasting our emotions and demeanor through our facial expressions, gestures, and body language. Even if we do not speak explicitly about our emotions, we communicate how we feel through nonverbal cues without realizing it, enabling us to form bonds and build rapport with other people.

Additionally, because emotionality is hardwired into our DNA by evolution, we are naturally very good at reading body language. Even if you consider yourself to be someone who cannot read nonverbal cues very well, you will be picking up on a wealth of information through subconscious processing. Without realizing it, you will be responding to the other person's body language, mirroring their postures, or forming opinions about your conversational partner's emotional state.

What this book has focused on, however, is how to process this information explicitly and act on it in an intentional, purposeful manner. Armed with this greater understanding, you will be able to act according to your conversational purpose, enabling you to have greater success in conversations and social interactions. Because human beings are so reactive to body language, even if we do not realize it, learning to control our body language and express the right emotion for the moment can have a profound impact on how we are perceived. Meanwhile, because people give so much away about their emotions, thoughts, and demeanor through their body language, learning to process these nonverbal cues in a purposeful way will provide a wealth of information that you can use to your advantage.

The key thing, however, is practice. As I have mentioned a few times throughout this book, interpersonal skills are like other skills and cannot be mastered through theory alone. To reuse an example, you would not expect to be a concert pianist after reading a book on piano theory. You need to put in the work to be a fantastic pianist, and, in the same vein, you need to put in the work to master interpersonal skills. Be confident in yourself, and do not feel as though you must apply every element of this book at once. Experiment with the tips and strategies and, as you improve, add another element to your growing repertoire. In time, you will start to see positive results from your hard work and perseverance. You will start to enjoy more career opportunities, more friendships, and more successful dating life.

However, this will take courage. You will have to put yourself out there and take chances. You will have to adopt a confident posture, even if you do not feel very confident, and find the strength to express your ideas forthrightly and passionately. On your journey, remember that you have something to offer the world. Be confident in your potential, find your inner strength, and bring change to the world around you in a positive manner.

GLOSSARY

- **Adaptive:** Beneficial to survival; see the evolution.

- **Affect:** A scientific term that measures both feeling and mood.

- **Behavior:** Any perceivable action.

- **Body language:** Any non-linguistic communication expressed by the body.

- **Chinese face reading:** A technique of traditional Chinese medicine that purports to diagnose emotional traits from the lines on a person's face.

- **Cognitive behavioral therapy (CBT):** A form of therapy that aims to regulate negative emotions by changing patterns of thought and behavior.

- **Cognitive cycle:** A central tenet of cognitive behavioral therapy (CBT) holds that behavior, sensations, thoughts, and emotions all have a causal influence on each other.

- **Conspec:** The theorized inbuilt capacity of the human brain to process and recognize faces.

- **Conversational purpose:** The intention and purpose behind a conversation.

- **Cortisol:** A stress hormone.

- **Deliberate versus spontaneous expression:** The difference between premeditated and automatic facial expression.

- **Demeanor:** The outward display of a person's purported emotions, displayed via behavior and body language.

- **Display rules:** The societal norms that determine how it is appropriate to express emotions in different cultures.

- **DNA:** Deoxyribonucleic acid, the main carrier of genetic information.

- **Emotional contagion:** The phenomenon by which emotion can spread from one person to another.

- **Evolution:** The scientific theory that holds that creatures with adaptive mutations are more likely to survive and procreate, thereby favoring adaptive traits over time.

- **Extrovert:** A person who takes energy from social interaction.

- **Eyebrow flash:** The brief rise and fall of the eyebrows, often indicative of a person's interest.

- **Facial expression:** Any body language displayed on the face.

- **Feeling:** The subjective experience of emotion.

- **Fusiform face area (FFA):** The area of the brain associated with high-grain differentiation associated with facial processing and recognition.

- **Intention:** The purpose or goal of a person's behavior.

- **Introvert:** A person who takes energy by spending some time alone.

- **Lateral occipital complex (LOC):** The part of the brain associated with processing and recognizing objects.

- **Mood:** A lasting emotion.

- **Musculoskeletal:** Refers to the muscles or skeleton.

- **Negative bias:** The evolutionary bias humans must recognize and process negative stimuli.

- **Pareidolia:** The common phenomenon of seeing faces in objects where no face is present.

- **Power pose:** A pose that produces a sense of confidence and power.

- **Proto-language:** A precursor to modern language.

- **Proxemics:** The study of the role physical closeness plays in social interaction.

- **Ripple effect:** The phenomenon by which an emotion or piece of gossip grows in intensity as it is spread across a group.

- **Similarity attraction effect:** The phenomenon by which we are more likely to prefer people who are like us in some way.

- **Testosterone:** A dominant hormone.

- **Stoicism:** An ancient Greek philosophy focusing on internal control of how we respond to life's events.

- **Voluntary hardship:** A stoic practice of voluntarily undergoing hardship to boost our physical and emotional resilience.

REFERENCES

Austin, A. (n.d.). *5 power poses to kickstart your confidence.* Poised & Professional. https://poisedandprofessional.com/2019/02/5-power-poses-to-kickstart-your-confidence/.

Barsade, S. G. (2002). The ripple effect: emotional contagion and its influence on group behavior. *Administrative Science Quarterly, 47*(4). DOI: https://doi.org/10.2307/3094912.

Benitez-Quiroz, C. F., Wilbur, R. B. & Martinez, A. M. (2016). The not face: A grammaticalization of facial expressions of emotion. *Cognition, 150*, 77-84. DOI: 10.1016/j.cognition.2016.02.004.

Clemente, J. (2020). *Former FBI agent explains how to detect lying & deception | Tradecraft | WIRED* [Video]. YouTube. https://www.youtube.com/watch?v=tpJcBozuF6A&ab_channel=WIRED

Cuddy, A. (2015). *Presence: bringing your boldest self to your biggest challenges.* Little, Brown Spark.

Damásio, A. (1994). *Descartes' error: emotion, reason, and the human brain.* Putnam.

Darwin, C. (1872). *The expression of the emotions in man and animals.* John Murray.

Ekman, P. (1972). Universal and cultural differences in facial expressions of emotions. In Cole, J. (Ed.), *Nebraska symposium on motivation* (pp. 207-282). Lincoln, NB: University of Nebraska Press.

Ekman, P. (1977). Facial expression. In Siegman, A. & Feldstein, S. (Eds.), *Nonverbal behavior and communication* (pp.97-116). New Jersey: Lawrence Erlbaum Association.

Elfenbein, H. A. (2014). The many faces of emotional contagion: an affective process theory of affective linkage. *Organizational Psychology Review 4*(4), 326. DOI: 10.1177/2041386614542889.

Frith, C. (2009). Role of facial expressions in social interactions. *Philosophical Transactions of the Royal Society B: Biological Sciences, 364*(1535), 3453-3458. DOI: 10.1098/rstb.2009.0142.

Edward-Elmhurst Health. (2019). *How emotions, like colds, are contagious.* https://www.eehealth.org/blog/2019/05/emotions-contagious/#

Hosseini-Koukamari, P., Ghaffari, M., Tavafian, S. S. & Ramezankhani, A. (2021). Using theoretical domains framework for exploring appropriate sitting posture determinants among office workers: a content analysis study. *Health Scope, 10*(1). DOI: 10.5812/jhealthscope.108354.

Humintell Admin. (2010). *The seven basic emotions: do you know them?* https://www.humintell.com/2010/06/the-seven-basic-emotions-do-you-know-them/

Isen, A. M. (Ed.). (1999). *Positive affect.* New York: John Wiley & Sons

Jack, R. E., Garrod, O. G. B., Yu, H. & Schyns, P. G. (2012). Facial expressions of emotion are not culturally universal. *Psycholog-*

ical and Cognitive Sciences, 109(19), 7241-7244. DOI: https://doi.
org/10.1073/pnas.1200155109.

Kamps, F. S., Hendrix, C. L., Brennan, P. A. & Dilks, D. D.
(2020). Connectivity at the origins of domain specificity in
the cortical face and place networks. *Proceedings of the National Academy of Sciences, 117*(11), 6163-6169. DOI: 10.1073/
pnas.1911359117.

Körner, R. & Schütz, A. (2020). Dominance or prestige: A
review of the effects of power poses and other body postures.
Social and Personality Psychology Compass, 14(8). DOI: https://doi.
org/10.1111/spc3.12559.

Koskowski, H. L., Cohen, M. A., Takahashi, A., Keil, B., Kan-
wisher, N. & Saxe, R. (2021). Selective responses to faces, scenes,
and bodies in the ventral visual pathway of infants. *Current Biolo-
gy, 32*(2). DOI: https://doi.org/10.1016/j.cub.2021.10.064.

Leder, T. (2018) *How to walk like a royal—how Janina Gavankar did
it* [Video]. YouTube. https://www.youtube.com/watch?v=ro9N-
qlMrdGY&ab_channel=LadyTinaLeder

Lee, D. H., Mirza, R. D., Flanagan, J. G. & Anderson, A. (2014).
Optical origins of opposing facial expression actions. *Psychological
Science, 25*(3). DOI: 10.1177/0956797613514451.

Marmolejo-Ramos, F., Murata, A., Sasaki, K., Yamada, Y., Ikeda,
A., Hinojosa, J. A., Watanabe, K., Parzuchowski, M., Tirado, C.
& Ospina, R. (2020). Your face and moves seem happier when I
smile. *Experimental Psychology 67*(1), 14-22. DOI: 10.1027/1618-
3169/a000470.

Miskandar, H. (2018). *Group of people doing jump shot photography photo* [Image]. Unsplash. https://unsplash.com/photos/FC4z3l-4sUYc

Obermair, C., Reiberger, W., Meschtscherjakov, A., Lankes, M. & Tscheligi, M. (2008). perFrames: Persuasive picture frames for proper posture. *International Conference on Persuasive Technology*, 128-139.

Park, S., Lee, S. W. & Whang, M. (2021). The analysis of emotion authenticity based on facial micromovements. *Sensors, 21*(13), 4616. DOI: 10.3390/s21134616.

Pease, A. & Pease, B. (1988). *The definitive book of body language: How to read others' attitudes by their gestures.* Orion Publishing Company.

Peterson, J. B. (2017). *Lecture 8: Neuropsychology of symbolic representation* [Video]. University of Toronto Maps of Meaning : The Architecture of Belief. https://www.youtube.com/watch?v=Nb5cBkbQpGY&t=0s&ab_channel=JordanBPeterson

Pogosyan, M. & Engelman, J. B. (2017). *How we read emotions from faces.* Frontiers for Young Minds. https://kids.frontiersin.org/articles/10.3389/frym.2017.00011

Schneck, A., Liu, S. & Lee, A. (2019). Posture wellness solutions in the workplace: a current review. *Journal of Ergonomics, 9*(3). DOI: 10.35248/2165-7556.19.9.252.

Straker, L., Abbot, R., Heiden, M., Mathiassen, S. E. & Toomingas, A. (2013). Sit-stand desks in call centers: associations of use and ergonomics awareness with sedentary behavior. *Applied Ergonomics, 44*(4), 517-522. DOI: 10.1016/j.apergo.2012.11.001.

Snyder, D. (2019). *Mind control skills: Face reading how to read anyone instantly through body language psychology* [Video]. YouTube. https://www.youtube.com/watch?v=MIllrWugvRw&ab_channel=Dr.DavidSnyder

Tez, A. (2019). *6 ways Jordan Peterson masters public speaking.* Medium. https://medium.com/the-mission/6-ways-jordan-peterson-masters-public-speaking-33fb3a488888

Thorp, A. A., Kingwell, B. A., Owen, N. & Dunstan, D. W. (2014). Breaking up workplace sitting time with intermittent standing bouts improves fatigue and musculoskeletal discomfort in overweight/obese office workers. *Occupational and Environmental Medicine, 71*(11), 765-771. DOI: 10.1136/oemed-2014-102348.

Tian, Y.-L., Kanade, T. & Cohn, J. F. (2005). Facial expression analysis. In Li, S. Z. & Kain, A. K. (Eds.), *Handbook of face recognition* (pp.247-275). New York, Springer. DOI: https://doi.org/10.1007/0-387-27257-7_12.

Van Edwards, V. (n.d.). *60 hand gestures you should be using and their meaning.* Science of People. https://www.scienceofpeople.com/hand-gestures/

Vacharkulksemsuk, T., Reit, E., Khambatta, P. & Carney, D. R. (2016). Dominant, open nonverbal displays are attractive at zero-acquaintance. *The Proceedings of the National Academy of Sciences, 113*(15), 4009-4014. DOI: https://doi.org/10.1073/pnas.1508932113.

Westside Toastmasters. (n.d.) *I have got to hand it to you.* https://westsidetoastmasters.com/resources/book_of_body_language/chap6.html

Wilkinson, N., Paikan, A., Gredebäck, G., Rea, F. & Metta, G. (2014). Staring us in the face? An embodied theory of innate face preference. *Development Science, 17*(6), 809-825. DOI: 10.1111/desc.12159.

Zabetipour, M., Pishghadam, R. & Ghonsooly, B. (2015). The impacts of open/closed body positions and postures on learners' moods. *Mediterranean Journal of Social Sciences, 6*(2). DOI: 10.5901/mjss.2015.v6n2s1p643.

Zumwald, T. (2019). *Do's and do nots: hand gestures when public speaking*. LinkedIn. https://www.linkedin.com/pulse/dos-donts-hand-gestures-when-public-speaking-teresa-zumwald#

Printed in Great Britain
by Amazon